A Short History of Virginia City

A SHORT HISTORY OF

Virginia City

RONALD M. JAMES
AND SUSAN A. JAMES

UNIVERSITY OF NEVADA PRESS — RENO & LAS VEGAS

University of Nevada Press, Reno, Nevada 89557 USA
www.unpress.nevada.edu
Copyright © 2014 by University of Nevada Press
All rights reserved
Manufactured in the United States of America
Design by Kathleen Szawiola

Library of Congress Cataloging-in-Publication Data

James, Ronald M. (Ronald Michael), 1955–
A short history of Virginia City / Ronald M. James and Susan A. James.
    pages   cm
Includes bibliographical references and index.
ISBN 978-0-87417-947-7 (paperback : alkaline paper) — ISBN 978-0-87417-948-4 (e-book)
1. Virginia City (Nev.)—History. 2. Comstock Lode (Nev.)—History. 3. Mines and
mineral resources—Nevada—Virginia City—History. 4. Virginia City (Nev.)—Social life
and customs. 5. Virginia City (Nev.)—Biography. I. James, Susan A. II. Title.
F849.V8J355 2014
979.3'56—dc23   2014008445

The paper used in this book meets the requirements of American National Standard for
Information Sciences—Permanence of Paper for Printed Library Materials, ANSI/NISO
Z39.48-1992 (R2002). Binding materials were selected for strength and durability.

This book has been reproduced as a digital reprint.

Frontispiece: The *Territorial Enterprise* staff and print shop occupied this fire survivor
after the 1875 disaster destroyed the newspaper's previous home. This building served as
home to the journalistic icon from 1875 to the mid-1890s. Lucius Beebe and Charles Clegg
purchased the structure and resuscitated the *Territorial Enterprise* as a weekly in the mid-
twentieth century. An outstanding museum in the basement exhibits an impressive array
of printing equipment. (Photograph by Ronald M. James)

Contents

Preface

Virginia City, the principal community of the Comstock Mining District, is the center of one of the first National Historic Landmarks recognized by the Department of the Interior. And for good reason. Some of the richest deposits of gold and silver in the world grant the district global significance. The Comstock participated in the transformation of the international mining frontier, when its focus shifted from placer mining—the washing away of dirt to expose gold nuggets and dust—to hard rock, underground excavations that placed an emphasis on corporate funding, salaried workers, and advanced planning by engineers. In addition, Comstock miners either invented or tested aspects of technology that dominated the industry for decades.

Virginia City has attracted tourists since travelers arrived in 1860 just to see the spectacle. Ever since then, "Comstock" has been a household word in the nation, if not the world. Even when there were economic slumps, something would happen to bring the district back to life, giving it a new role in the dreams of people who imagined wealth or who simply loved the mystique of the Wild West. In the twentieth century, visitors began trekking up the mountain to see the famed mining camp as it seemed about to drift into the realm of the ghost towns. But Virginia City survived and greeted the postwar world with a new vigor made all the stronger after 1959 by the fictional Cartwrights of the television series *Bonanza.*

No matter the decade, visitors have found a magical charm about the Comstock that refuses to die. The area repeatedly performs in surprising ways. While preserving a pivotal chapter in world history, the district continues to live as a thriving community with a character undiminished by the century and a half since the first mineral strikes. At the same time, it can be difficult to sort out what one is seeing when walking along the boardwalks of Virginia City or along the old unpaved paths that wind across the mountain. Sorting out the past and how it folds into subsequent decades—and into the present—is a challenge.

With this in mind, we offer a short history of Virginia City together with a walking tour. This volume is not the first history written about the town and surrounding area, but it is an attempt to provide a concise account in a way that is immediately accessible. Strolling along in the small community that hugs the side of Mount Davidson, it is difficult to imagine a time when this town, built in an improbable location, lured people from all over the world. In its heyday, the Comstock was a noisy, bustling industrial center where more than twenty thousand people lived and worked in houses and businesses crammed side by side. The district was filled with the twenty-four-hour racket that went along with the extraction and crushing of ore. Stagecoaches and wagons pulled by teams of horses added to the din. Culturally sophisticated, Virginia City rivaled San Francisco for its diverse entertainments and cuisine, and its public buildings were touted as the finest on the Pacific Coast. Masses of humanity moved along the boardwalks, and languages from all over the world could be heard on the streets and in the saloons, restaurants, and hotels.

Since the prosperous 1860s and 1870s, there have been times when Virginia City settled into a quiet period, but it has never lasted long. Today, visitors arrive for many reasons. The Old West has its own allure, but there are still some who are enthusiastic because of the Comstock's ties to the legendary TV show *Bonanza*. Others are delighted to learn that Virginia City also contributed to the development of a particular genre of rock and roll in the 1960s. Each decade has left its mark and represents a tale to be told. After giving hundreds of tours of Virginia City, during which we have shared the story of this remarkable place, we found good reason to put down in writing what we have described in person to thousands of visitors, placing in print what has previously been a matter of discussion.

With the experience of nearly four decades of working with Comstock material, we are in a position to acknowledge some outstanding institutions that make research into the history of the mining district possible. The Storey County Recorder's Office has made tremendous leaps forward in record management and digitization. Its vault is filled with documents that tell the story of how the Nevada Territory and then the state first organized, emerging as an economic powerhouse in the nineteenth century. Thanks are owed to a long succession of elected county recorders and their dedicated staffs.

In addition, the Nevada Historical Society, the Special Collections at the University of Nevada–Reno Library, the Historic Fourth Ward School Museum, and the Comstock Historic District Commission all profoundly contribute to everyone's understanding of the Comstock Mining District. These are valuable institutions that help define what Nevada is and what it means to be a Nevadan. The same is true of the University of Nevada Press. Senior acquisitions editor Matt Becker was pivotal in inspiring this volume, but everyone at the press played a crucial role, contributing unique talents that made this book possible. They have our thanks.

A Short History of Virginia City

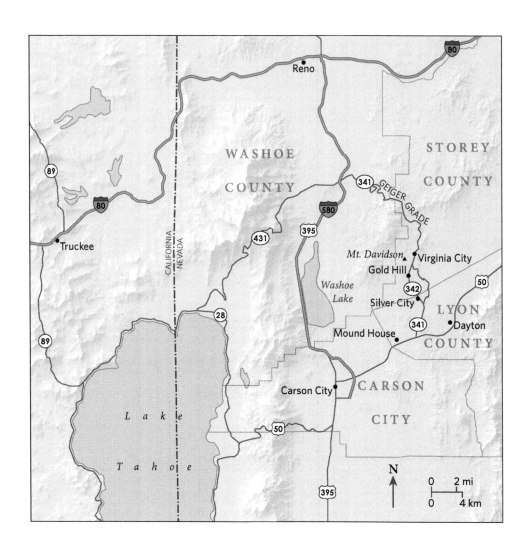

Introduction

During the nineteenth century, Virginia City won recognition as the location of one of the largest gold and silver strikes of all time. Internationally, people have claimed that any one of dozens of mines was the "richest place on earth," but the Comstock's assertion of that distinction is close to legitimate. Established in 1859, the Comstock Mining District remained productive for twenty years and continues to yield into the twenty-first century. During its nineteenth-century boom period, the district produced well over $300 million in precious metals, but today that figure would equal something in the billions of dollars.

Virginia City—the largest community of the Comstock—survives as one of the West's more popular tourist attractions. At more than fourteen thousand acres, the district is one of the largest National Historic Landmarks, and hundreds of buildings allow visitors to imagine a past in the most intimate of ways. Still, the town that welcomes people by the hundreds of thousands does not always make clear what is being seen. Decades of occupation have created a cacophony that assaults the visitor, who might have difficulty distinguishing between the historic and the new. That having been said, the idea of dividing the place between the modern and the old is far too simple. Each generation left an imprint on the district: the original period of mining had several distinct phases, and then in the twentieth century Virginia City reinvented itself several times, with each episode affecting it.

Famed Western photographer Carleton Watkins captured Virginia City during an 1878 visit, five years after the discovery of the Big Bonanza had propelled the Comstock to lasting international fame. Huge mine dumps of worthless shattered rock shine brightly in an industrial landscape, pointing uphill to the deep shafts that regurgitated the debris. Mount Davidson rises 1,600 feet above tightly packed houses, businesses, centers of industry, and the newly opened Fourth Ward School to the far left. (Courtesy of the Comstock Historic District Commission)

Adding to the complexity of the place, the population of the Comstock has also changed repeatedly over the years as fortune seekers have come and gone, and periods of boom—*bonanza,* to use a popular Spanish term of the day—yielded to times of decline, or *borrasca,* again drawing on a Spanish term that was well known at the time. When the prosperity of the mining district waned, residents struggled financially and often left for better opportunities. As a result, Virginia City is both one of the best-preserved historic districts in the West and a place that has been in constant flux. Providing stability to the economy and local culture, the Comstock has had some sort of gold and silver mining in every decade. At the same time, generations of residents have presented their past in different ways as they repeatedly readjusted to life on the steep slope of Mount Davidson.

Within this confusing context, several routes lead to an understanding of the Comstock. First of all, it is a place of enormous wealth. Without its valuable ore, the slope of Mount Davidson would be devoid of residents, like thousands of other mountains in the Great Basin. The fame that the Comstock Mining District has enjoyed for more than a century and a half is tied to a body of ore that has yielded more gold and silver than almost any other place in the world.

The reality that the abundance of precious metal was locked underground in a remote location demanded new technologies and investment in an extensive infrastructure. The mining district can consequently be considered to be a center of innovation. From flat wire cable and the underground use of dynamite to early experiments with air-compressed drills, the Comstock became the proving ground for cutting-edge technologies. This, combined with the fact that the district required the development of an infrastructure including roads, railroads, and a water system that brought water some twenty-five miles from the Sierra, caused Virginia City and its environs to be celebrated as the ultimate expression of the industrial ingenuity, strength, and progress of its time.

The legendary wealth of the Comstock attracted an international population, and its ethnic diversity is yet another way to consider the history of the district. People from throughout the world settled there, helping to give Nevada, for a while, more foreign-born residents per capita than any other state in the nation. Chinese immigrants, banned from work underground, built a sizable Chinatown, working in the residential neighborhoods as laundrymen, servants, and cooks. But there were also thousands of Europeans, Canadians, Mexicans, and people from Central and South America. Local newspapers described an ongoing calendar of festivals and celebrations associated with the various groups who had come to call the Comstock home. Fraternal organizations and businesses addressed the needs of these diverse residents. To walk the streets of Virginia City was to encounter dozens of languages. It was an international capital of industry.

Some of the more notable figures of the century came to the Comstock. Because Virginia City was a tourist attraction from the start, many visitors stayed for only a few weeks. Others lingered longer, and the Comstock placed its imprint upon them. So many accomplished writers worked there that a literary movement, the Sagebrush School, is named for them. The most famous is Samuel Clemens, who became Mark Twain while living in Virginia City. Many others added to the pantheon of people who passed through and either were prominent or would acquire fame, regardless of the decade. This process did not cease with the 1880s, the time of the first major slump in mining production.

The Comstock became and has remained famous for what it achieved as much as for the riches uncovered there. Technological innovation, a magnet for immigrants, and a tourist attraction from the start—each represents one way to understand the Comstock. Today, the historic district commemorates an extraordinary past, but unlike a place such as Williamsburg, Virginia City and its sister towns are not locked in time. They are living communities that change even while they preserve history.

Perhaps the most remarkable thing about the mining district is the way Comstockers have repeatedly sought to reinvent themselves, surviving and adjusting as they endured the challenges of each new decade. The landscape of the West is littered with abandoned ghost towns that whisper of failed dreams. Virginia City residents met declining fortunes with adaptation. The longevity of the first phase of mining was no doubt a factor: few districts could claim twenty years of outstanding productivity. Many left with the first major decline, but a significant number remained, hoping for the best or refusing to leave a place that had been home for so long. Flexibility was key to survival. Whether it was as a bohemian colony of artists and writers during the 1930s and 1940s, an emerging tourism attraction in the 1950s, or the location of experimentation that helped found the unique psychedelic rock-and-roll sound of San Francisco, Virginia City adapted. With the premiere of the television series *Bonanza* in 1959, the Comstock became the focus of a tidal wave of visitors who wanted to see the place where the Cartwrights lived, even if the story of this family was entirely fictional. Fourteen years later, the program ended, and the nature of Comstock tourism began to change. Once again, Virginia City wrapped itself around a new reality, writing its most recent chapter as residents reconsidered what it means to live in the historic district.

This volume offers a history of how Virginia City grew and changed over time. It also describes the people who caused this amazing story to unfold. The Comstock has contributed to the mining industry of the nation, and at the same time, its residents have explored various ways to profit from a harsh environment. The story is complex and often contradictory. The goal here is to offer a portrait of a place and its past, presented in an approachable way.

Chapter One

The Beginning of a Legend

In 1849, Abner Blackburn traveled across the western Great Basin as part of the famed Mormon Battalion, which had participated in the California revolt against Mexico. Blackburn tried his hand at placer mining with the sands of a creek that flowed from the north into the Carson River. With good fortune, he found a gold nugget. The place would forever be known as Gold Canyon, and Blackburn did not forget the discovery. Traveling on, he soon realized that the western Great Basin held many possibilities. He returned to his original strike, began working the local sands for "color," and took to trading.

Some three hundred miners eventually earned respectable livings with a primitive level of technology that involved shovels and wooden boxes called long toms and rockers where worthless dirt could be washed away, leaving heavier bits of gold to be picked from the remains. For several years in the early 1850s, placer mining thrived along creek beds throughout the region. Unfortunately for these hardworking laborers, gold-bearing sands were finite, and after depleting the deposits, many left for other prospects. By the late 1850s, those who remained considered going higher into the ravines, ascending what would later be called the Virginia Range.

There was a remarkable sideline to this story that would hint at the great things to come. In 1853, Pennsylvania natives Allen and Hosea

Grosh crossed the Sierra after traveling to the Gold Rush. A Portuguese miner named Frank Antonio claimed that he and some other prospectors had discovered a rich vein of silver, and the Grosh brothers wanted to see what they could find. While surface deposits had attracted the attention of nearly everyone else, the deeper geology of the western Great Basin intrigued a few others. In fact, millennia-old faults had provided the pathways for water to travel far into the earth and then to return as mineral-laden steam. By chance, gold and silver dominated what nature brought from below, leaving random pockets of wealth along the system of fractures. Where the deposits had erupted at the surface, flakes of gold washed down into the ravines. While the placer miners of the 1850s retrieved these remnants, they had only a superficial understanding of the geological processes that created this opportunity.

The primordial violence that lifted the Sierra and shook the land with earthquakes and volcanic eruptions left the mountains of the Great Basin rich in minerals but too often starved of soil. The resulting composition of the Comstock Lode is such a complex interplay of faults, convulsions from deep within the earth, erosion, and uplifting planes of rocks that its exact nature remains a matter of controversy. The most recent, twenty-first-century phase of mining has added new insights into the structure of the system that brought riches from deep below, challenging conventional wisdom and asserting a new way to consider the region. Whereas earlier geologists saw the Comstock Lode as mineralization along a single, nearly straight fault, there is now good evidence—thanks to extensive drilling associated with exploration—that the Comstock fault line is one of several parallel fractures in the earth's crust. And rather than trending in a straight north-by-northeast line, it is actually an arc extending north of present-day Virginia City, sweeping south beneath what is now Gold Hill, then turning gently in a curve to the east, passing beneath Silver City and beyond.

Because the underground ore erupted to the surface in a few places, erosion caused gold to wash into creek beds, attracting the attention of early prospectors. Unlike those interested in working for gold in stream beds, the Grosh brothers sought veins—and in particular deposits of silver—descending underground. Sands filled with gold dust and nuggets along washes could provide a good living, but pursuing subsurface ore bodies offered the best chance to attain greater prosperity. The brothers crossed the Sierra twice more to study what they believed was a "monster vein" of silver, describing their efforts in letters sent home to their father. But in 1857, during their last trip, Hosea struck his foot with a pickax and died of the subsequent infection. Devastated by the loss of his brother, Allen decided to return to California, but he and a friend were caught in a November snowstorm. Allen died from exposure, after writing a last letter recounting his fate.

The Grosh brothers had almost certainly failed to discover a deposit of significance. Still, their story would become part of local legend, and their insight, that something of great significance lurked below, anticipated the future. Regardless of what they did or did not find, life in Gold Canyon continued as placer miners struggled to eke out a living from increasingly scarce deposits along the creeks that descended from what they called Sun Mountain.

The Comstock Lode was first discovered in January 1859 in what would be known as Gold Hill. On June 8, 1859, another strike, this one at the future site of Virginia City, set the stage for the region to gain international fame. According to local lore, that evening Henry Comstock rode into the camp of Patrick McLaughlin and Peter O'Riley to assert his claim to a share of the ore. (Courtesy of the authors)

In January 1859, a few miners hiked to the head of Gold Canyon and found an outcropping of ore that nature had broken down, making it easy to process with the crude equipment of a placer miner. Between winter storms, these intrepid souls excavated the crumbling rock, retrieving more gold than many had found while working for years in the creek beds below.

Later in the spring, two Irish immigrants, James McLaughlin and Peter O'Riley, ascended the mountain range from the east, leaving behind the exhausted gold-bearing sands along what would be called Six Mile Canyon. On June 8, 1859, searching high on the slope, the two miners found a spring, which they decided to dam so they could use the water to wash dirt in search of gold. While working on the project, they threw some of their back pile into a rocker, and at once they saw that the soil was rich with the precious metal.

Laboring through the day, O'Riley and McLaughlin were able to retrieve several ounces of gold. As they were closing their operation at dusk, a local prospector named Henry Comstock happened upon them. He recognized the value of their discovery and asserted that they were trespassing on his property. The two wanted to avoid conflict, so they offered Comstock part of the claim, which he immediately insisted should be shared with his partner, Emanuel "Manny" Penrod. What today sounds like claim jumping was a common enough practice for a time when fluid ownership created and dissolved partnerships. And there was an advantage to having more partners: contemporary custom allowed for the ownership of additional feet with every new member of the company.

Throughout June and into July, various small camps of miners worked where the ore breached or came near the surface, retrieving a great deal of gold. At the same time, they complained that a heavy blue mud was gumming up their efforts to wash soil because this material was nearly as heavy as the gold and it was difficult to separate the two. In late June, one of the claimants took a sample to Grass Valley, California, to have the material assayed. The lab found that a ton of the ore would produce more than eight hundred dollars or nearly three and a half pounds of gold. The real surprise, however, was that it would also yield in the neighborhood of three thousand dollars or roughly one hundred and seventeen pounds of silver. It was an astounding discovery. Everyone was sworn to secrecy, ensuring that word spread quickly.

Within days, hundreds began scrambling over the Sierra to stake claims. For reasons that are not entirely clear, the new mining district took its name from the fast-talking Henry Comstock. The ore was called a "lode," using a term borrowed from Cornwall, where miners had worked underground for centuries. Thus, propelled by news of the wealth it was yielding, the Comstock Lode became well known throughout the nation in a matter of months.

A sudden surge in population changed the remote mountain, but this was only the first of many early Comstock transformations. Within weeks of the 1859 strikes, the initial claimants—the placer miners who were now working the newly discovered outcroppings of underground ore—began selling to investors, who made up a second wave of enthusiasts. Locals often referred to these people as "California rock sharps," suggesting they were fools with too little knowledge and too much money. The original miners probably thought they had exhausted the richest ore, and if that were not the case, they had certainly removed most of the easily reached gold and silver. When someone arrived willing to pay thousands of dollars for a claim that may have been depleted, the choice seemed clear. One by one, nearly all of the first claimants sold their interests in the Comstock for what seemed like a fortune, not realizing that they were giving away millions.

Among the early entrepreneurs who bought a claim was a thirty-eight-year-old Missouri native named George Hearst. He obtained part of the Gould and Curry Mine. As it turned out, he had had the good luck to purchase an interest in what would become one of the more lucrative operations. After a few years of making a great deal of money, Hearst sold his share for what tradition maintains was more than one hundred thousand dollars, which he took to a succession of other western mining districts until he had the multimillion-dollar foundation of the Hearst empire. He died in 1891 as a U.S. senator representing California, a success story with a Comstock foundation.

The fame of the Hearst fortune aside, most arrived in the mining district humble but hopeful. And most left without much to show for their efforts. One story dating to 1859 has taken an honored place in

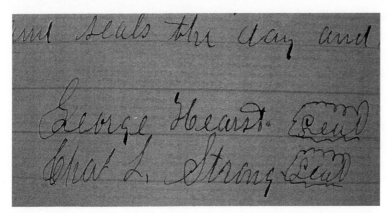

The names George Hearst and Charles Strong, officials of the Gould and Curry Mine, are recorded as part of a land transaction documented in Virginia City on May 14, 1860. Hearst used the wealth of the Comstock to launch a career that catapulted his family into the American aristocracy. (Courtesy of the authors)

local folklore, in part because of the way it depicts the modest circumstances of many who landed there in the first few months. In response to the promise of wealth, Dublin-born John Mackay and his partner, Jack O'Brien, crossed the Sierra and walked to Virginia City. Mackay would later tell how O'Brien asked if his companion had any money. When Mackay replied that he had none, O'Brien reached into his pocket for his last half dollar, which he flung into the sagebrush and declared that they would enter the new mining camp as equals and gentlemen. There is no way to tell if this anecdote is true, but the way it has become embedded in local tradition speaks volumes about how Comstockers viewed—and continue to view—their earliest roots.

As the multitudes arrived, most settled into two communities close to where the lode erupted on the steep slope of Mount Davidson. The earlier town to the south quickly became known as Gold Hill, taking its name from the mound of ore that protruded from the southern face of the mountain. A second settlement was organized after the June strike on the eastern elevation of the range. The name of this place remained a matter of debate for several months. Some favored Ophir, after the fabled lost gold mine of Solomon celebrated in the Old Testament. Others thought its name should honor Chief Winnemucca, a respected leader of the region's Northern Paiutes. Ultimately, the collection of tents and shacks became known as Virginia City, a designation entwined in legend that, once again, may or may not be grounded in truth.

James "Old Virginny" Finney, his nickname taken from his native state, was one of the early placer miners in Gold Canyon. He participated in the first discoveries of the Comstock Lode, and being a likable fellow with few, if any, enemies, he was a camp favorite. It is possible that local miners simply settled on naming their new town in his honor without anything more than affection to inspire the choice. There is, however, a story that continues to reverberate throughout the region. It seems that Finney drank to a degree that impressed even his peers, a group known to enjoy alcohol. One night, as the tale goes, Finney was staggering back to his tent, drunk and carrying a half-empty bottle of whiskey. He stumbled and broke the bottle. Finding only a bit of the precious liquid left in what remained of the glass, he declared that he would not let it go to waste. Finney poured the last of the spirits on the ground and proclaimed that he was baptizing the new camp "Virginia City." Whether or not the story is true, the name of the largest and most prosperous community of the Comstock Mining District came to honor the affable prospector and his home state.

Silver City was another town that sprang up as a consequence of the 1859 strike. Founded on a minor deposit of ore below Gold Hill, Silver City exploited the fact that it was a good place to establish a toll station on the southern access to the larger Comstock communities uphill. On the north side of Silver City, two prominent rock walls pinched Gold Canyon to a small opening, known as Devil's Gate. The route that became a well-used, privately constructed highway had to cut through this narrow opening, and it was an obvious location to charge travelers for the use of the road. Businessmen quickly built toll stations coming in and out of Silver City. Today a remnant of the original toll station may be seen just south of Silver City, where metal sticks out of a rock face on a road supported by a crude stone wall along Gold Creek.

Farther to the southeast, Dayton grew into a substantial center of milling and commerce, but this town emerged before the 1859 strikes. This was Nevada's first permanent emigrant habitation, dating to 1850 when it served as the home base for the earliest placer miners working in Gold Canyon. To this day, there is a dispute with Genoa, to the southwest at the foot of the Sierra, as to which place deserves the title of Nevada's oldest community. Genoa had a post office and other hallmarks of a town before Dayton, but the latter was apparently the first to have year-round inhabitants. Consequently, it is possible to assert that while Genoa is Nevada's first town, Dayton is the region's oldest European American settlement.

Situated at the confluence of Gold Canyon Creek and the Carson River, Dayton was in a perfect position to play an entrepreneurial role for the early miners and for the subsequent Comstock Mining District. The community was originally called Chinatown because it had a number of Asians living there, but residents changed its name by 1861 in honor of John Day, a local surveyor. Although the town eventually added the milling of ore to its services, Dayton never achieved the size or fame of Virginia City or even its lesser satellite, Gold Hill.

During the summer and fall of 1859, Virginia City and Gold Hill expanded quickly as new arrivals set up makeshift shelters including tents and dugouts in the side of the mountain. Most residents probably wondered if the mining district would survive, since the short cycle of boom and bust was well known in the West. Smaller colonies organized in places like the Flowery Mining District, a few miles to the east, down the canyon from Virginia City. These, too, took the form of crude camps. The difference was that Gold Hill and Virginia City had a future that included substantial buildings, but for that first year, it was impossible to know what would unfold. And the winter, which was more severe than usual, must have made many question whether they should linger. With spring, however, hundreds more poured over the Sierra, and with them came the means to start erecting permanent structures. Wooden buildings, and then some of brick and stone, were soon scattered across the hillside. The Comstock's tent cities quickly transformed into enduring places. And more importantly, production of gold and silver bullion increased. In fact, underground work demonstrated that the deposits were larger than anticipated.

Almost as soon as Gold Hill began to take shape, a Scottish immigrant named Eilley Orrum Cowan settled there and took in boarders, served meals, and washed clothes to accommodate some of the hundreds of men arriving in the area. Newly separated from her second

Author-artist J. Ross Browne visited the Comstock in the early 1860s on assignment from *Harper's Weekly*. His depiction of the settlement below Virginia City known as the Flowery Mining District captures the rustic early life of tent-dwelling miners. Two miners turn a wheel that is used to lift and lower men, tools, and ore from a shaft. The Flowery diggings ultimately failed to yield much by way of valuable gold and silver. (Courtesy of the authors)

husband, Cowan needed a source of income. Tradition maintains that the first women in the mining camps of the West were prostitutes, but there is no actual evidence that they were anything but hardworking entrepreneurs pursuing respectable occupations. There were so many ways a woman could make a living that there was little reason to resort to sexual commerce. Cowan recognized an opportunity and exploited it. According to local folklore, when one of her boarders lacked cash, he paid with ten feet of a Gold Hill claim.

A Missouri-born miner named Sandy Bowers, who was working in Gold Hill, owned the ten feet next to Cowan's. The two came to know each other and found common interests expressed both in business and then in marriage. She was thirty-three, and he was twenty-nine. Unlike most of the early claimants, the Bowers couple held on to their property. As it turned out, they owned one of the richest near-surface deposits, making them two of the first millionaires on the Comstock.

The crescendo of prosperity and optimism seemed unending until an incident in the spring of 1860 caused everyone to wonder if success did, indeed, have its limits. The local Northern Paiutes were increasingly frustrated by the new arrivals, who killed game and cut down pine groves, the source of nuts that were the Native Americans' means of winter sustenance. For thousands of years, the first inhabitants of the Great Basin had been adapting to a changing environment that had become increasingly harsh. Scarce resources did not support large populations, but those who lived there thrived, dependent on a nomadic life as they exploited seasonal resources and then moved on to the next opportunity. At one time or another, the Northern Paiutes and the neighboring Washoe claimed the mountain slope that would serve as home to Virginia City, but the resources there were so scarce that apparently neither tribe gave the area much attention. The fact that Northern Paiutes settled in Virginia City once it was established suggests that in the decades just before contact they may have dominated the general region more than the Washoe did.

Local American Indians encountered newcomers for several years before placer miners worked Gold Canyon in the 1850s, but most often, the Paiutes and Washoe merely watched as people passed through on their way to the Pacific Coast. When hundreds and then thousands arrived to stay, however, the dynamic shifted.

A flash point occurred when some men operating a nearby station on a trail captured two Paiute girls and held them as sexual slaves. Relatives tracked down and rescued the captives, slaying their abductors. The reaction on the Comstock was swift, with no consideration of the reason for the killings: there was a call to teach the Paiutes a lesson. More than one hundred volunteers headed north to Pyramid Lake on May 12, 1860. The ragtag group of Americans encountered a well-planned resistance that took advantage of the terrain. The Paiutes knew their land, and they defended themselves with expert tactics and fighting skills. The day ended in a rout with the bodies of more than seventy Comstockers littering the path back to Virginia City. Panic gripped the mining district.

Dr. Edmund C. Bryant, a relative of American poet William Cullen Bryant, was heading toward Virginia City just as the trouble erupted. The New York native wrote his father on May 31 that "I met trains of people and stock on their way to California, flying from the Indians." Since his father-in-law was already on the Comstock, Bryant continued on his way to Virginia City and volunteered to treat the wounded. For those who stayed, defense was the top priority. A newly erected stone building in Virginia City became a fort, housing the few women and children who lived in the community. To the south, Silver City's militia occupied one of the rock bastions of Devil's Gate. They fortified the lookout and fashioned a wooden cannon, which they filled with powder and metal objects. It was fortunate that it was never fired in anger, for when it was finally tested, the cannon exploded and would have killed anyone standing nearby.

In spite of the panic and all the preparations, the Comstock never received the anticipated attack. The Paiutes just wanted to be left alone, but that was not to be. A force of regular troops and more than five hundred volunteers arrived from California and began a march toward Pyramid Lake to confront the Paiutes on June 2, 1860. Skilled warriors were able to slow the assault on their home long enough to evacuate the women, children, and the elderly, and then they too slipped away into the northern waste. But it was summer, and without a good source of water or food, there was no choice except to sue for peace. The short-lived Pyramid Lake War came to an end, and the first chapter of the area's Native American struggle for fundamental human rights was over.

What had inspired some to leave the Comstock turned out to be only a minor setback, and with peace at hand, the rush resumed stronger than before. At least a few who arrived as volunteers stayed. Dr. Bryant, who had written of the chaos in the war-stricken territory, fetched his wife,

Marie Louise, and his daughter from California. Similarly, two brothers, Thomas and Robert Gracey, aged twenty-one and eighteen respectively, had volunteered after the first battle. The Graceys came from Downieville, California, but they had only recently emigrated from the Isle of Man in the Irish Sea. They, too, became part of the human tempest, the coming and going in response to the crisis. Like Dr. Bryant, they found reason to stay. Each had a story that became entwined with those of the thousands of others who came to call Virginia City home.

The Comstock society that emerged was different from what might have been imagined in the summer of 1859. In just a few months, the district had evolved into something new. It began as a place where fortune seekers wanted the chance to strike a claim and develop it with a few associates. According to the dream, hard work and good luck could produce millionaires, or at least enough money to head east and buy a farm. By the summer of 1860, a different sort of Virginia City had taken root. This was now a mining district where a single poor prospector had little opportunity to strike it rich. Instead, corporate owners paid wages to laborers. The wealth of the ore body meant that everyone did well, but there was a big gap between an owner who commanded thousands, if not millions, and a wage earner who made $3.50 per day. It was remarkable pay for the time, but it was not the path to financial independence.

With that transformation, the dream that had fueled the California Gold Rush of 1849—the vision that was behind the first sprint to the Comstock—became harder for the everyday worker to achieve. That is not to say that many did not try. Indeed, there is ample evidence of wage-earning miners chasing elusive bodies of ore during off hours with their own excavations over the course of the following decades. A few actually did well, but as the labor force of underground workers swelled into the thousands, it became clear that true wealth was not likely to be gained with the strength of one's own back. And while many purchased stock, attempting to escape the ranks of labor through investments, that game of chance was too often rigged by the corporate owners who manipulated prices and took advantage of information that only an insider could have.

Whether as owners or laborers, those who participated in the first season of mining in Virginia City wondered if the rush would last several months, another year, or longer. Most probably assumed the diggings would follow the typical California example, where miners abandoned a region after exhausting its surface deposits. There were, however, indications that this was something different. The first hint was the depth of the ore. Initially, miners used open pits to reach into the earth and scoop up the wealth, but within a few months, the sidewalls threatened to collapse and workers found they would need to pierce the ground with shafts.

Soon after the 1859 strikes, Comstock miners faced three types of challenges, but a crisis on each of these fronts was delayed until the spring and summer of 1860. The development of deep mines, the demand for supplies, and the need for cost-effective milling of ore each presented problems, and those who would build a world-class industrial giant needed to arrive at solutions. The first crisis came in the field of mining. For thousands of years, people had ventured underground to retrieve the various minerals the earth offered, but the Comstock Lode presented its own unique problems, and underground mining, in general, is a death sentence for anyone lacking the knowledge to pursue the craft correctly.

Excavating underground transformed the West, replacing self-employed placer miners with wage-earning shifts of industrial workers, a labor force that required a large outlay of corporate funds. A range of machinery added to the cost, often before the first ore was processed: steam engines were needed to pump out water, frequently found in boiling pockets, to circulate air, and to hoist men and equipment up and down shafts while lifting worthless rock and valuable ore from the depths. In the first months of probing underground, Comstock companies relied on established technology, but the cost alone demanded a level of financial support that had rarely been needed in the West before that time.

The first serious technical issue to challenge miners was the size of the Comstock's vein of ore. This was not a bad problem when it is remembered that the deposits were extraordinarily rich in gold and silver. Miners in most districts were thrilled if the width of a gold vein could be measured in inches. The Comstock Lode, however, saw the size of the ore body fluctuate from a narrow slip of precious metal to an expanse that had to be measured in feet. In fact, at the greatest breadth, the deposits were forty, fifty, and sometimes as much as sixty feet. The resulting "stope," as miners referred to the area left behind when hollowed out for the retrieval of ore, was too large to be supported by spanning timbers. No log, regardless of thickness, could span a dozen or more feet while holding up a mountain of rock and soil without snapping.

Philipp Deidesheimer, a German engineer educated at the Freiburg School of Mines, arrived at the solution to this problem. Born in 1832 in Darmstadt, Hesse, Deidesheimer was in his twenties when he came to Virginia City in late 1860. The superintendent of the Ophir Mine summoned him to consider ways to handle the width of the Comstock Lode and the fact that the surrounding rock often proved too unstable for traditional supports. After studying the predicament for several weeks, the engineer invented a modular system that became known as square-set timbers. The plan was perfect for Virginia City. Although square sets were soon widely used in the neighboring mines and eventually throughout the world, Deidesheimer failed to patent his invention, and he never received compensation for his revolutionary design.

Deidesheimer's device called for stout timbers, twelve by twelve inches and five to six feet long, with ends notched in such a way that when they were assembled into a cube, they would lock in place. Because the cubes could be connected one after the next and also stacked upon each other, the innovation allowed miners to support a variety of openings with a solid structure that would not collapse. Floorboards could be added to the cubes so work might be shifted in any direction and at any height. Diagonal timbers enhanced the strength of the configuration. Ultimately, miners would hoist worthless debris only as far as the more recently-emptied stope and backfill it, giving further stability to that area. The invention made the retrieval of the enormous Comstock deposits possible, and its importance cannot be overstated.

The widespread use of square-set timbers immediately underscored the next problem that the Comstock would need to tackle, namely the logistics of supporting a remote mining district and community. Many who later visited the Comstock noted that each excavation had the appearance of a large church, with the shaft taking the part of the steeple and the sprawling mine below, completely supported by wood, assuming the role of the body of the building. Most importantly, the mines

Philipp Deidesheimer, a German-trained engineer, invented the square-set timber method in 1860 as a way to support the Comstock mines. The modular approach was safe and easy to manufacture, making it the industry standard, internationally, for the next half century. (Courtesy of Eugene Hattori)

demanded an enormous quantity of straight, high-grade lumber, and Mount Davidson had next to none.

The closest forest covered the Sierra Nevada range, which at its nearest point was a dozen miles to the west. The implementation of Deidesheimer's invention required the emergence of a lumber industry, which began with the cutting of roads. In addition, gangs of lumberjacks would need to work the mountains to feed the mines. And it did not end there: entrepreneurs had to construct mills to cut the logs, and teamsters were needed to haul the lumber to the mining district. Comstock corporations would have to pay for all these efforts, even before they employed an army of carpenters to assemble the square sets.

Roads served the need to import other things as well. Food, clothes, iron, and tools all had to come from somewhere else. In addition, Comstock workers wanted their beer, whiskey, and wine. The building of an infrastructure, essential for the community's survival, was an immense undertaking. The task is often overlooked in spite of the pivotal accomplishment that it represented, for without the ability to deliver much-needed supplies and raw materials to the Comstock, the development of the mines would have been impossible.

The third issue that needed to be addressed—the milling of ore—resulted in yet another indication that the Comstock represented something permanent. The first miners had constructed arrastras, simple structures introduced by Mexicans who exploited animal labor and the warmth of the sun. These round platforms had stone floors and walls, with a center wooden post. The miller tethered a horse or mule to the post and placed ore on the stone floor of the arrastra. Then the animal dragged a large rock over the ore, breaking it apart. The miller subsequently stirred in water, salts, and mercury, leaving the sun to heat the mixture. The mercury combined with the gold and silver, which separated and sank to the bottom of the concoction for easy removal.

There was, however, a need for an industrial solution to process ore that did not depend on warm, sunny days. Almarin Paul constructed one of the first steam-operated mills on the Comstock in 1860. This approach consisted of a first stage in which ore was hammered by a stamp mill. Steam power turned a crank that lifted and dropped a number of heavy pistons to pulverize rock into powder. Paul then placed this material together with water, salts, and mercury into a large metal cauldron that was heated with steam, a source of power that also turned a paddle to keep the contents mixing. Through trial and error, he and others improved what became known as the Washoe pan process. This perfected the breaking down of the silver ore, which in its natural state was chemically bonded with other elements and was difficult to retrieve. At the final stage of the process, both the gold and the silver, now free, combined with mercury to form an amalgam that could be cooked to drive off the mercury, leaving only precious metal. Common practice failed to recover all of the silver and gold, but the mills, with their constantly clanking stamps and their rows of metal vats, were effective enough to make the Comstock profitable.

Yet another challenge that Comstock mines faced was water. Building ever-larger pumps was generally the way engineers handled the problem, and some of the machinery—together with flywheels of gargantuan proportions—became legendary in the community. There were some engineers who conceived of drainage tunnels, an approach made practical by the fact that the mines descended from the slope of a mountain and there were low points that could serve as horizontal access to passively drain the mines. Taking advantage of the geography, four north-end mines, the Mexican, the California, the Central, and the Ophir, joined forces in 1860 to dig what they called the Union Tunnel. Begun in June and finished the following October, the excavation was 1,100 feet long and cost about $10,000. It intersected with the mines at the 200-foot level, so it was quickly made obsolete as shafts descended to much lower depths.

One of the first to advocate the use of an even deeper and longer drainage tunnel was Adolph Sutro. The child of Prussian Jews, Sutro immigrated to North America in 1850 at the age of twenty, quickly going to San Francisco. In 1856 he married Leah Harris. With the opening of the pass over the Sierra in March 1860, Sutro arrived in Virginia City. Recognizing the value of a tunnel to provide a passive drain for the mines, he began advocating for ever-longer adits to intersect with the mines at increasingly deep levels. His grandest proposal was for a tunnel that would be more than three miles long, extending from the Carson River valley to drain the Comstock mines at the 1,660-foot level. On February 4, 1865, he organized the Sutro Tunnel Company to pursue this dream, but actual work was delayed and the ramifications of his proposal are part of subsequent chapters of the Comstock story.

Before the mining district was a year old something else happened that would hit on a theme of growing importance to Virginia City: tourists began to arrive. During the winter of 1860, J. Ross Browne, an Irish-born author and illustrator working for *Harper's Weekly*, waited on the western slope of the Sierra for the first opportunity to cross into the Great Basin. He shared the trek with the second wave of fortune seekers who wanted a chance to capture the wealth flowing into the new towns thanks to the ore erupting from the ground. But Browne was after a treasure different from gold and silver: he wanted a good story. And he found it. He walked over the mountain pass that reached the south shore of Lake Tahoe in March between snowstorms and finally made his way to Virginia City. A community that had grown by the hundreds before winter snow closed the passes in late 1859 was now swelling by the thousands. Many arrived and left almost as quickly. By the time the federal census enumerators recorded the district in the summer of 1860, there were more than three thousand residents in Virginia City and Gold Hill.

Browne's pen provided one of the earliest portraits of the Comstock, in both words and images. He described a primitive place filled with the coarsest of men—and a few women. Virginia City was an assault on the senses. In defiance of the harsh landscape, a shantytown had taken root on the muddy eastern slope of Mount Davidson, where unwashed dregs occupied every filthy tent and rocky outcropping. According to the author, brawling was the main form of entertainment, with plenty of whiskey to fuel disputes over mining claims. Browne concluded that Virginia City in its infancy was grim. Accommodations were failing to keep up with demand. Food was substandard, and drink was too often poisonous. As far as he was concerned, there was really nothing to recommend the place except the promise of wealth. As Browne wrote, "This district is said to be exceedingly rich in gold, and I fancy it may well be so, for it is certainly rich in nothing else." Finally, the end of his trip was as revealing about Virginia City as any description. The water was so vile it made the traveling author sick, and he left in disgust.

In October 1860, the British explorer Sir Richard Francis Burton passed through the Great Basin. He had just wrapped up his African expedition to find the source of the Nile River. Seeking a tamer adventure, Burton decided to explore the Church of Jesus Christ of Latter-day Saints, the new religion that had found a home in Utah. As he headed back to the Pacific Coast, he could not resist visiting the mining district that was capturing the world's attention. The account of his adventure, *The City of the Saints,* does not tell historians much about Virginia City. But with his sketch pad in hand, Burton depicted a maturing Virginia City while standing on the edge of the growing Ophir Pit, the glory hole that was yielding millions in profits. His single drawing of the place lacks details and appears absurdly pastoral. Yet Burton's arrival and his interest in the Ophir Mine speak eloquently of the time. It is clear that even as early as 1860, Virginia City was gaining a reputation for remarkable wealth, and travelers were drawn to see the spectacle.

The Comstock provides a bookend for the mining of the Far West. Just

VIRGINIA CITY.

J. Ross Browne drew one of the earliest portraits of Virginia City for his 1860 article about his visit to the Comstock. (Courtesy of the authors)

as the '49ers had opened the region to placer mining conducted by small groups of unskilled, self-employed laborers, the Comstock initiated the era of deep hard-rock mining. There were western places other than Virginia City that explored underground, but the mining district set the standard for the industry, and its wealth and innovations captured headlines. These new efforts required skill, technology, and corporate investment to support salaried miners, equipment to sustain and de-water a mine, and mills to process the ore. Because of the Comstock's remote location, the logistics of procuring lumber, supplies, and food and water for the emerging community also had to be addressed. Virginia City and the Comstock Lode became the prototype for deep precious-metal mining and for building a town and its infrastructure in an inhospitable environment. For the next fifty years, throughout the world, the industry would follow the Virginia City example.

That is how it is possible to understand the mighty Comstock Lode as it fit into the largest international context. But there were also the stories of the people, some of whom thrived as others failed in this harsh environment. Dr. Bryant, who had arrived in the midst of the Pyramid Lake War, stayed to open a practice. Before long, he developed an addiction to alcohol and opiates. The physician died in 1866, leaving his family in poverty. The following year, his widow, Mary Louise, married an emerging mine owner who had proven he was a hard worker with the gift of good luck: it was none other than John Mackay, who had entered the mining camp in 1859 without a penny to his name. Within a few years of his marriage, Mackay became one of the richest silver barons in the world. Marie Louise Hungerford Bryant Mackay—who was born in Brooklyn, raised in California, and widowed in Virginia City only to remarry there—would eventually hold court in the elite social circles of London, Paris, and New York.

The cycle of boom and bust played out differently for Sandy and Eilley Bowers. In 1862, the couple used several hundred thousand dollars of their fortune to erect a mansion in nearby Washoe Valley, itself booming with some of the earliest mills for processing Comstock ore and others cutting Sierra lumber. A lengthy trip to Europe in search of elaborate furnishings further depleted their wealth. They returned to the most splendid residence in the Nevada Territory and a mine with an exhausted body of ore. Sandy died of lung disease in 1868, and their young daughter, Persia, succumbed six years later. Eilley lost her mansion, and spent the rest of her life trying to make ends meet telling fortunes as the "Washoe Seeress." She died, destitute, in 1903.

For the Gracey brothers, the young immigrants from the Isle of Man who had arrived as the Pyramid Lake War unfolded, the Comstock provided modest success. Thomas became the Storey County assessor and the Virginia City constable during the territorial period. The brothers opened a prestigious saloon and returned frequently to their beloved place of birth. There, they married Manx women and came back to the Comstock as established family men. Their descendants continue to live in the area.

Philipp Deidesheimer, the engineer who made the full development of the Comstock Lode possible with his square-set timbering, settled in Virginia City with his wife, Matilda. Unfortunately, lightning was destined to strike only once. Deidesheimer's subsequent attempts at investing in profitable mines led to nothing of significance. Mine owners often sought his association with their enterprises because having his famous name on their masthead could lend credibility to an operation, boosting the price of stocks. But too often it was the ploy of less-profitable businesses.

Profiles of a few of the thousands who arrived show how diverse Virginia City was from the start. Irish, Germans, Manx, Scots, and many others mingled with those born in the States and Canada and with those who spoke Spanish. At the very beginning of the organization of the Comstock Mining District, a few Chinese immigrants and African Americans added to the ethnic kaleidoscope. Taken as a whole, the newcomers with all their diverse backgrounds affected the lives of the Native Americans in the area, who looked on as their world forever changed. For good or ill, the Comstock grew from a remote outback into a center of industry, boasting towns that were capturing the attention of the world.

Chapter Two

An Early Boomtown

Three years after his first visit in 1860, J. Ross Browne, the correspondent working for *Harper's Weekly,* decided the Comstock still had viable literary ore available for excavation. In late 1863, he observed that "perhaps there is not another spot upon the face of the globe that presents a scene so weird and desolate on its natural aspect, yet so replete with busy life, so animate with human interest." With the genius of a literary master, Browne went on to capture the full depth of the Virginia City of this time:

> Steam-engines are puffing off their steam; smoke-stacks are blackening the air with their thick volumes of smoke; quartz-batteries are battering; . . . subterranean blasts are bursting up the earth; picks and crow-bars are picking and crashing into the precious rocks; shanties are springing up, and carpenters are sawing and ripping and nailing; store-keepers are rolling their merchandise in and out along the way-side; fruit venders are peddling their fruits; wagoners are tumbling out and piling in their freights of dry goods and ore; saloons are glittering with their gaudy bars and fancy glasses, and many-colored liquors, and thirsty men are swilling the burning poison; auctioneers, surrounded by eager and gaping crowds of speculators, are shouting off the stocks of delinquent stockholders; organ-grinders are grinding their organs and torturing consumptive monkeys; hurdy-gurdy girls are singing bacchanalian songs in bacchanalian dens; . . . bill-stickers are sticking up bills

of auctions, theatres, and new saloons; newsboys are crying the city papers with the latest telegraphic news; stages are dashing off with passengers for "Reese"; and stages are dashing in with passengers from "Frisco"; and the inevitable Wells, Fargo, and Co. are distributing letters, packages, and papers to the hungry multitude. . . . All is life, excitement, avarice, lust, deviltry, and enterprise.

With journalistic giants like Browne and Sir Richard Burton having a look at the Comstock, no one was likely to take note when a luckless, failed gold miner came to Virginia City in September 1862, also hoping to strike it rich with his pen. While the trips of Browne and Burton were of note, the arrival of this other fellow, a twenty-six-year-old named Samuel Clemens, was not. In spite of Clemens's lack of notoriety at the time, his Comstock sojourn would prove to be far more important for the nation's literary landscape. Ironically, the reason that Clemens was even in Nevada had nothing to do with the craft of writing. Instead, it rested in the realm of national politics and also in the very roots of the mining district itself.

Throughout 1860 and into the following year, people from every inhabited continent arrived in Virginia City and its neighboring communities. Congress had plenty of reasons to look after the wealthy newborn region, because there was a general perception that the Comstock needed to be protected from the Utah territorial government. Members of the Church of Jesus Christ of Latter-day Saints—or Mormons, as they were called—established a community in the eastern half of the territory. They had threatened to seize the federal land they inhabited, proclaiming it the independent state of Deseret. Washington's concerns over the hint of secessionism and over the Mormon practice of polygamy inspired an 1857 occupation by federal troops. Congress was consequently suspicious of the Utah Territory.

The discovery of the Comstock Lode added another reason to deprive Utah of some of its real estate and power. Leaving a massive deposit of gold and silver in the hands of the Mormon Church might result in mischief should the federal government be distracted—as it soon was—by the rebellion of the South. In addition, the Mormon Church discouraged precious-metal mining because of the industry's potential to inspire non-believers to flood into a region. In general, San Francisco corporate owners and investors wanted something other than a Mormon government east of the Sierra, and non-Mormon miners would chafe under the government in Salt Lake City. Congress sought a territorial government that would encourage mining, would remain staunchly loyal to the Union, and would satisfy popular demand from San Francisco to Virginia City.

As one of his last acts, in March 1861 President James Buchanan signed the bill that gave Nevada independent territorial status. It was up to the newly inaugurated president, Abraham Lincoln, however, to appoint the government officials. Lincoln rewarded James Nye, a political ally from New York, with the position of governor of the new territory. He then selected a supporter from Iowa named Orion Clemens to serve as secretary/treasurer. In an accident of history, Orion's younger brother was looking for the chance to leave his home along the Mississippi River. With the outbreak of the Civil War, Sam Clemens feared that since he was an experienced riverboat pilot, the Union might draft him for his services. Besides that, he wanted adventure, and Nevada, with the reports of its fabulous gold and silver mines, seemed like the perfect place to visit.

While Orion's brother hoped for employment with the new territorial administration, government resources were scarce, and Sam was forced to pursue other options. He tried his hand at developing a timber claim in the Lake Tahoe Basin, and he worked as a miner in Unionville to the north of the Comstock and in Aurora to the south. All of the younger Clemens's attempts at finding fortune through hard labor failed, but he met some success with a few letters sent to Virginia City's newspaper, the *Territorial Enterprise,* signing his witty observations "Josh." Joseph Goodman, the publisher, liked the author's work and offered him a job as a salaried reporter late in the summer of 1862.

Samuel Clemens arrived in Virginia City in September 1862 and left in May 1864 after taking the pen name Mark Twain. This image dates to a few years later, after he began his transformation from witty journalist to famed American author and lecturer. (Courtesy of the Library of Congress, LOT 13301, no. 8)

The twenty-six-year-old was a natural storyteller, having learned the craft from white and black raconteurs on the banks of the Mississippi in his native Missouri. In Virginia City, Clemens was introduced to the western tradition of the tall tale, adding a new ingredient to the resources at his disposal.

Comstock editors and reporters were fashioning rival newspapers—and in particular the *Territorial Enterprise*—into respected institutions, but they occasionally indulged in writing pieces designed to hoodwink readers into believing a preposterous anecdote. A noted practitioner of this form of literature was Clemens's mentor: William Wright wrote serious mining reports as well as tall tales for the *Enterprise*. Signing his work Dan De Quille ("Dandy Quill" as well as "Dan of the Pen"), he called the hoaxes "quaints," but regardless of the term, they were a natural offspring of the West. The critical component of this genre was that the piece had to have enough subtle flaws so that a reasonably critical reader would understand that it was not true. The art of the telling was to dupe most of the readers, not with an outright lie but with a story that flirted with the boundary between fabrication and absurdity.

Clemens took to the idea as though he were a native son of the Pacific Coast. Over the course of a year and a half, he learned the ropes and began writing under the pen name Mark Twain. The name was apparently a reference to two fathoms, which in riverboat parlance means barely safe and very near to trouble. The Comstock was transformative. It turned poor miners into millionaires, and it changed a down-on-his-luck vagabond into a literary shooting star.

The Virginia City that Clemens encountered in 1862 had undergone a remarkable transition during the previous two years. As the mines continued producing millions of dollars in gold and silver, the community grew in size and complexity. It had quickly transformed from a town of tents and dugout shelters in 1859 into a fully established city. By the summer of 1861, people were erecting substantial buildings along the commercial corridors of B and C streets as well as wherever mines had sunk shafts or entrepreneurs erected mills. A town plan solidified, with streets traversing the hillside and others taking traffic up and down the steep slope. African American artist Grafton T. Brown captured the community and its more significant structures in a bird's-eye view published in early 1861.

Virginia City was extraordinary in many ways. First, it had defied the odds, given that most mining boomtowns grew up and then disappeared in a matter of months. The community celebrated its third birthday in 1862, and its mines were still yielding breathtaking amounts of precious

Grafton T. Brown, an African American artist noted for his western landscapes, captured Virginia City in late 1860 or early 1861. He documented a town that was established and growing. Wooden and masonry buildings, some two and three stories, rise above busy streets. The church near the lower right corner was probably the one built by Methodists. (Courtesy of the Library of Congress, LC-USZ 62-7743)

metals. Even more extraordinary was the enormous effort it took to sustain a town with thousands of residents in the barren interior of the Great Basin. The mines, mills, and new buildings of brick, stone, and iron were impressive and becoming more common.

While a few fortune seekers stand out in the history of the Comstock Lode, most who arrived in the early years made their living working at a wide range of jobs that allowed the community to thrive and prosper. By 1862, Virginia City boasted dry goods stores, restaurants, fire companies, and of course the newspapers, which employed people such as Wright and Clemens. There were doctors and dentists as well as musicians, jewelers, and blacksmiths. A local brickyard produced much-needed material for masonry, and construction workers representing a full range of skills found employment. Sensing that the mining boom was not a fleeting event, some brought their wives and children. At a minimum of

$3.50 per day during those first months of prosperity, Comstock miners claimed to be the highest-paid industrial workers in the world, and they wanted the best education for their children. Small private schools, often little more than a room in a house, were scattered throughout the district, but these were quickly followed by the construction of public schools in each of Virginia City's four voting districts. Teachers were so much in demand that institutions often suspended the traditional prohibition against allowing married women in the classroom.

Industry required the ability to forge whatever the new engine of progress needed. Among the several foundries that took root on the Comstock hillside was a company organized by John McCone, an Irish immigrant who came to the Comstock in 1862. His Pioneer Foundry was perfectly positioned to provide critical parts for the machinery of mines and mills. Finding himself in the midst of fellow Irish immigrants, McCone joined the local chapter of the Fenian Brotherhood, which dedicated itself to the emancipation of Ireland from British rule. In Virginia City, however, the Fenians were much more than revolutionaries. They organized the earliest units of the Nevada National Guard. They drilled under the flag of the United States, but it was British targets they imagined during shooting competitions. McCone was typical of these immigrants for whom patriotism meant loyalty to both Ireland and their new American home. He served as a stalwart member of the community until his death in 1876 at the age of forty-six.

In spite of his premature departure from the Comstock stage, McCone's story did not end at that point. His descendants continued in the family business: his grandson and namesake, John Alexander McCone (1902–1991), played an important role in the steel industry on the West Coast. In 1937, he merged his interests to form the Bechtel-McCone Company, and the new corporation became one of the largest producers of Liberty ships for the Pacific Theater during World War II. The younger McCone went on to have an impressive career in public service as well, eventually being appointed director of the Central Intelligence Agency under President John F. Kennedy. McCone subsequently became the center of conspiracy theories involving the president's assassination because he was a Republican, but his party affiliation was a natural by-product of his Comstock roots. While most Irish immigrants to the United States became Democrats, those who settled in Virginia City were typically Republicans: the Comstock was so fiercely pro-Union during the Civil War that joining the Grand Old Party was the only practical choice.

Local foundries like John McCone's may have produced much that was needed in the mines, but still more had to be imported. Virginia City's growing populations required even more food—and beer, whiskey, and wine—than before. But that was not all: mercury by the ton and large amounts of salts and other chemicals were vital to the milling process. Teamsters brought preformed parts for buildings but also raw materials that included lumber, glass, iron, wallpaper, and paint. All of this arrived using a steadily growing system of roads, which functioned like the arteries of a gigantic body. Beyond these highly traveled routes, an extensive network of smaller capillaries extended throughout the region, reaching east and west for even more remote resources. For lumber, trails extended deep into the Sierra, north and south, providing paths to haul massive, old-growth logs from distant groves to mills. There, workers cut centuries-old timbers into Deidesheimer's square-set posts, while other logs were transformed into lumber of standard building sizes for the structures aboveground.

Virginia City was no longer a canvas boomtown. It was a capital of industry, wealth, and enormous expectations. And all of this meant that a growing system of reliable roads was replacing the crude wagon trails that emigrants from the 1840s and 1850s had traced across the continent. In the first years, only a few roads linked Virginia City with the outside world. They crossed the Virginia Range to the west so teamsters could haul ore for processing and return with supplies from Washoe Valley and from the lumber mills located in the area of Washoe Lake. Heading east from Virginia City, wagons traveled downhill along Mill Street, a thoroughfare used to reach even more ore-processing sites and then eventually leading to the Carson River, downstream from Dayton and extending to the hinterland of the Great Basin.

A route to the south through Gold Hill and Silver City veered to the southeast to reach Dayton, and once connected with the trail along the Carson River, led west to Carson City and beyond. And to the north, travelers to and from Virginia City used what is now known as the

Lousetown Road, heading to the Truckee River and its east-west transcontinental emigrant trail.

All of these roads followed fairly obvious paths that required little by way of engineering and construction. In 1861, Dr. D. M. Geiger proposed a route to the north that would be the most ambitious of all. The territorial legislature granted him a franchise to build the road and charge those who would use it. Opened in 1863, Geiger's Grade, as it was known, reached the valley to the west near Brown's Station and Steamboat Springs. Travelers could then follow an easy course north to Lake's Crossing, the bridge that spanned the Truckee at a place that would later transform itself into Reno. This route became the principal means to leave Virginia City to the north, growing more important over the decades as Reno increased in significance. As an unpaved road, however, Geiger's Grade did not age gracefully. Old Comstockers could recall how early in the twentieth century, Geiger's road diminished into a bed of mud in the winter and spring, leaving ruts fossilized with the heat of summer. Fortunately, the Works Progress Administration provided funds for the road to be re-engineered in 1936. Geiger Grade emerged paved, and its steepest climbs and tightest turns were reworked into the gradual winding ascent that one finds today. But it is also possible to see some of the old road. At one of the last hairpin turns on the way to Virginia City, there is a place to pull off and explore, to see how the 1863 route turned deep into the ravine, crossing the drainage with an old stone bridge. That structure was bypassed during the Great Depression by a massive earthwork that supports the highway around a gentler curve.

With the emergence of the Comstock in the early 1860s, the region's new roads witnessed the arrival of even more specialized provisions. Items ranged from food and fabrics to books, newspapers, medicines, and hardware. Everything that residents of a vibrant community needed or wanted had to be imported. Oyster beds all along the Pacific Coast, from the San Francisco Bay to Seattle, furnished the popular delicacy. Cattle arrived from California. Ale and white clay tobacco pipes can be traced to Glasgow, Scotland. The Duchy of Nassau, in today's Germany, sent its mineral water. Perfume arrived from France. But there was more: red clay pipes originated in the American South, and a bottle of Tabasco Pepper Sauce indicates that this condiment improved Virginia City cuisine within a year or two of the 1868 invention of the sauce on Avery Island, Louisiana. China and even Japan contributed enormous amounts of material to satisfy the needs of a growing Comstock population from the seven counties of Guangdong, better known to the English-speaking world as Canton. Until local businesses could meet demand, San Francisco Bay Area foundries contributed dozens of heavy iron pilasters, the half-column I-beams that tied together the fronts of masonry buildings. Wagons carried these and other metal castings the two hundred miles that separated the Comstock from the coast. Fabrics and dress patterns, from as far away as Paris, meant that the small but growing number of women could don the latest fashions while strolling along Virginia City's streets or sitting on furniture manufactured in England or on the Atlantic Seaboard. Day after day teamsters rolled into town by the dozens, bringing even more products from nearly every continent.

The Comstock's hardworking population craved diversions, and a few entrepreneurs found profit in their abilities to provide entertainment. German immigrant John Piper was one of the hardy souls who arrived in Virginia City in 1860, remaining for nearly four decades, until his death. The former fruit stand operator joined the "Rush to Washoe" from San Francisco with his wife, Louisa, and brothers, Joseph and Henry. Instead of a barren wasteland, they saw a community brimming with opportunity. While Virginia City's drinking water had sickened J. Ross Browne, John Piper turned the situation to his advantage. He quickly opened his Old Corner Bar, a place where patrons could purchase beer, liquor, or fine wine for a "bit"—twelve and a half cents—per glass. Piper's saloon became his springboard to a remarkable career that eventually included management of the local opera house and a stint as mayor and state senator.

The young mining town attracted representatives of a diverse range of professions. Typically, those who engaged in sexual commerce watched from their homes in other communities, waiting to see if the boom would turn to bust. As Virginia City gave all of the signs of lasting more than a few months, prostitutes relocated there throughout the 1860s. Madams Cad Thompson, Jenny Tyler, and Jessie Lester established brothels in the D Street entertainment district. Their businesses offered upscale surroundings to customers and a relatively safe workplace for the young women they employed. Julia Bulette and Gertrude Holmes were independent operators who lived and worked from tiny houses on the northeast corner of D and Union Streets, in a neighborhood where many prostitutes rented their places of business from John Piper. Bulette and Lester met the violent fate of so many in their profession, but only one was destined to become a legend, a story that unfolded in a later chapter of Comstock history.

The federal manuscript census documents a wide variety of occupations, opening the door to imagination: street musicians and gymnasts performed for a fluid pedestrian audience around the town, while formal theatrical institutions existed nearly from the beginning. As stages were erected, actors provided the Comstock with sophisticated performances, and there was even a "temple of comedy." The community had to wait until 1863, however, for something monumental with regard to the dramatic arts. Thomas Maguire prepared to debut a grand opera house to rival his well-known establishment in San Francisco. He opened his Virginia City hall on July 3 while the battle of Gettysburg raged in Pennsylvania and as Vicksburg fell, securing Mississippi for the Union. The nation's best acts premiered that summer on McGuire's fifty-foot-wide stage with the greatest stars of the time: Julia Dean Hayne (America's

San Francisco theater impresario Tom Maguire opened his opera house in Virginia City in 1863. Its front business block appears here, rising behind a row of C Street businesses. The photograph, taken from the International Hotel in 1866, also captured the Episcopal church. (Courtesy of the Library of Congress, LOT 3544-48, no. 715)

darling of the 1860s), well-known character actor Walter Lehman, Frank Mayo (who would make the role of Davy Crockett famous), and Junius Brutus Booth, Jr. the eldest brother of the famed acting family. The grand opening of Maguire's was such an important event that Mark Twain rushed back from San Francisco to see the curtain rise for the first time. Reviews raved about the facility as well as the plays it featured. And all this happened within feet of brothels to the north and the belching steam engines running the hoist works for the mines, just to the south.

And there was "some talk of building a church," wrote Mark Twain a decade later, reflecting on his sojourn in his delightful book, *Roughing It*. Of course, reading the nation's favorite satirist requires skepticism, and as is so often the case, a wonderfully funny line does not reflect the truth. Many Comstockers craved a religious word or two, and there is ample evidence of supply meeting demand from the start. Reverend Jesse Bennett, who tended to a Methodist congregation in Carson City, is credited with preaching the first sermon in Virginia City in 1859. It was an impromptu event on C Street. According to tradition, the response was several hundred dollars in silver, gratitude from spiritually starved residents.

By 1860, Father Hugh Gallagher erected the first Catholic church in the community. Early in 1861—a year and a half before the arrival of Samuel Clemens—Grafton Brown's bird's-eye view of Virginia City depicted a church with a tall spire on what appears to have been D Street, perhaps in the location where the Methodist church once stood. That same year, Rev. Henry O. G. Smeathman gave the town's first Episcopal sermon, and plans to erect a building for that faith developed, with the doors opening in early 1863. Those edifices soon stood as symbols of how the community sought to project a moral image. Other congregations including the Baptists, the Presbyterians, and the African Methodist Episcopalians—the last specifically for African Americans—organized, and eventually boasted their own structures. But that was not all.

Even though they never had their own temple, the growing Jewish community was holding religious services in various places within a few years of the 1859 strike. And during that same time, the Chinese immigrants built a joss house, which functioned as a temple, community center, and administrative headquarters. By 1864 a group of monks had established a monastery on the south end of town and the Daughters of Charity arrived to begin their work with children. So in spite of Twain's witticism, it is apparent that Virginia City residents quickly expressed an interest in attending religious services. As the *Mercantile Guide and Directory for Virginia City, Gold Hill, Silver City and American City* was able to indicate in 1864, "One of the strongest proofs of the intelligence, growth and progress of Virginia, lays in the towering steeples of the many churches that dot the city on every side. Perhaps in no city in the United States has a people thrown together from all parts of the world, in such a short space of time, boasted of so many churches and places of worship for the population."

The churches, however, were not nearly as impressive as the individuals who brought religion to this transforming part of the West. Although names like Bennett, Gallagher, and Smeathman occupy important places in the first chapter of Comstock religious history, others are etched more vividly in the Virginia City story. Franklin S. Rising, Ozi W. Whitaker, and Patrick Manogue provide three examples of ministers who played crucial roles in the unfolding of the community. Rising, the Episcopal priest, dedicated the original church of his denomination in 1863. He and his brother, the district judge in Virginia City, were important to the foundation of society in the first years after the community was established, although Rev. Rising's contribution was cut short by retirement due to ill health in 1866. Massachusetts native Rev. Whitaker replaced him, and in 1869 Whitaker became the missionary bishop for Arizona and Nevada while continuing to serve the parish in Virginia City. Reno residents will recognize his name because of its association with a park in northwest Reno, originally the home of an Episcopalian school for girls that Whitaker opened in 1876.

Of the religious pioneers on the Comstock, Patrick Manogue was destined to become the most prominent. Born in Ireland in 1832, Manogue immigrated during the 1846 Potato Famine and subsequently made his way to the California gold fields. There, the giant of a man—he was six feet three inches tall—worked as a miner. When he raised enough money to pursue his dream of a life in the clergy, he traveled to Paris to study for the priesthood at the Saint-Sulpice Seminary. After ordination in late 1861, Manogue returned to the American West. Bishop Eugene

Part of a panorama of photographs dating to 1866, this view of Virginia City shows three churches: the Episcopal (left) the Catholic (center), and the Methodist (intruding at the far right side of the frame). (Courtesy of the Library of Congress, LOT 3544-48, no. 714)

O'Connell of Grass Valley, California, subsequently sent him to Virginia City to tend to its new parish. Father Manogue quickly began building a new church, which was dedicated in 1864. Although he would construct another, see it destroyed in the fire of 1875, and then rebuild on the foundation of its predecessor, Manogue's contribution surpassed the erection of churches. The priest quickly became a bulwark of faith and morality in the mining district. With Virginia City's growing Irish immigrant population, Manogue was naturally inspirational for much of the community. Known as *Soggarth Aroon*—Gaelic for "Beloved Priest"—he exhibited a kindness and a sense of even-handedness that caused his influence to be felt far beyond those of his faith. Manogue was the most highly regarded of the nineteenth-century ministers who practiced on the Comstock, and he remains celebrated while the names of the others are barely remembered.

The cast of characters who pursued material wealth on the Comstock varied as much as the joss house attendees differed from the celibates at the monastery. Many recognized that selling products and services to the community represented a quick path to profit, and hundreds of people lived comfortably in Virginia City or left with fortunes of one size or another without venturing underground. For those who looked to the mines, there were several options, and their choices typify the opportunities during this early period. Experience and wisdom taught that most truly successful mining districts flashed brightly for a brief moment and then faded. The difference between a successful area and one that was legendary could be counted in the dozens of months of longevity. While Comstock wealth seemed extraordinary, by the beginning of 1863, the district was pushing the bounds of life expectancy. When the mines faltered later that year and into early 1864, many shrewd players believed they saw the signal to leave.

In anticipation of the failure of the Comstock, George Hearst sold his interests and left to invest in other emerging mining districts of the West. Similarly, when the Maldonado brothers realized that their north end property, the Mexican Mine, had all but exhausted the obvious ore, they pursued other opportunities. The Spanish-speaking brothers—who used traditional Mexican mining technology—mortgaged their mine to build the large Mexican Mill in Washoe Valley. The Maldonados then sold the entire business for a profit, leaving new owners to discover that valuable ore was gone and the mine supports were sparse and near failure: shortly after the sale, the mine collapsed, diminishing its value and damaging the neighboring Ophir.

Sandy and Eilley Bowers might have done well to sell their claims, but they hung on when others left. John Mackay represented a third possibility. Possessing the agility of Hearst, he nevertheless believed there was still potential in the Comstock mines. Unlike Sandy and Eilley Bowers, however, Mackay was quick to move from claim to claim. When he suffered setbacks, he nimbly redirected his efforts within the district, always ready to explore and exploit new possibilities. While Hearst used that strategy throughout the West, Mackay accomplished the same goal without having to relocate. In most other mining districts, Mackay's approach might have failed. But he was lucky: the Comstock had an unprecedented amount of wealth in its vaults.

As the mines faltered in 1863, the owners of the International Hotel followed Hearst's lead, but in much more dramatic terms. Teamsters hauled the wooden structure to Austin in central Nevada, more than a hundred miles to the east. A new mining district had opened there, and it seemed promising. Ultimately, Austin was a poor gamble. Another surge in the Comstock mines justified rebuilding an even larger, brick

International Hotel in 1864. This incarnation burned, as did its 1877 replacement, the victim of a fire in 1914. The sequence of disasters ironically meant that the only surviving expression of the International Hotel, this most important of Comstock institutions, is now the modest wooden edifice in Austin.

Like Mackay, John Piper never gave up on Virginia City. When an 1863 fire destroyed his Old Corner Bar, Piper purchased real estate across the street on the northwest corner of B and Union, where he constructed a brick business building known as the Piper Block. His new Old Corner Bar, now housed in the substantial structure, continued to prosper. Always interested in profitable ventures, Piper looked to Virginia City's raucous D Street entertainment district. He purchased Maguire's Opera House in 1867 and enhanced its role as a required stop for actors traveling on the national theater circuit. Piper's D Street auditorium became the first of three Virginia City opera houses that made his name legendary among theater managers of the West.

Under Piper's management, his stage achieved national importance in the history of the American theater. Besides being an essential place to perform throughout the rest of the nineteenth century, meaning that dozens of notable actors, musicians, and lecturers graced the stages of his auditoriums, the surviving facility is also a remarkably well-preserved expression of period theater technology. In addition, Piper's theater is

Yet another image from 1866 features the International Hotel, on the northwest corner of C and Union Streets. The structure burned in the Great Fire of 1875 and was replaced with an even grander hotel. (Courtesy of the Library of Congress, LOT 3544-48, no. 711)

noted as the place where theater impresario David Belasco, often called the "Bishop of Broadway," passed an important chapter at the beginning of his career.

Belasco (1853–1931) was a young actor earning his stage chops when he worked for Piper in the 1870s. Years later, he wrote about those early days, recalling how Piper was a benevolent employer, but he also encouraged his performers to gamble and run up bar tabs at his Old Corner saloon. Belasco, who did not drink, knew it was good politics to patronize his boss's establishment, and soon found himself tied to Piper by a large debt. When he tried to skip out on the obligation, the sheriff brought him back to Piper, who advised him to give up such foolishness.

Over the course of thirty years, Piper's personal life reflected the highs and lows of the mining district, and Belasco found himself in a front-row seat during one of the unhappy episodes. Piper's wife, Louisa, suffered from mental instability, which the theater owner attempted to manage in their Virginia City home. Belasco later recalled that Piper took him in during a brief illness, and he often heard the miserable woman's cries as he regained his strength. One night, Belasco was startled awake to see Louisa, in a rage, standing over him. Despite her violent threats, he and a caregiver were able to soothe her, and a disastrous situation was averted. Belasco went on to a legendary career on Broadway. Unable to care for Louisa at home, Piper ultimately had her committed to the Nevada State Hospital, where she died in 1925.

Regardless of regional economic downturns and the fires that destroyed his theaters, he always rebuilt. Late in Piper's career, John Mackay stepped in with financial aid as the theater impresario struggled to erect and maintain yet another opera house. Piper died in 1897 at the age of sixty-six, but the institution he created still entertains patrons at the corner of B and Union.

Ultimately, so much of what one made of the mining West came down to luck. The noteworthy cases of prosperity—too often followed by economic failure—are well known in a way that is disproportionate to the thousands who dreamed big and never acquired anything more than a reasonable salary working underground.

While much of Comstock history followed the all-too-familiar rise and fall of mines and the subsequent economic turmoil in people's lives, Virginia City has always had a knack for the unpredictable and the remarkable. A magical event occurred during Christmas of 1863, and it continues to affect American literature into the twenty-first century. Beginning in 1858, Charles Farrar Browne had earned a name as America's premier humorous journalist, and he eventually laid claim to the title of one of the nation's first standup comedians. Browne performed as a result of financial practicality: writing as Artemus Ward for *The Plain Dealer,* a newspaper in Cleveland, Ohio, he had no way to profit when other newspapers reprinted his work, even though they were making him nationally famous. In 1862, he published a collection of his columns, titling the volume *Artemus Ward, His Book.* It was an instant success, but Ward continued to be plagued by those who pirated his writing. He fell on the idea of giving stage presentations under his invented persona, charging for his performances and exploiting new venues to sell *His Book.* In 1863, he took his act to the West, where he hoped to gather material for a subsequent volume he would call *His Travels.*

Ward arrived in Virginia City at the end of 1863. As a newspaperman, he immediately fell in with the local journalists. He quickly gravitated to Dan De Quille and Mark Twain, sharing their apartment during his stay. Although his visit lasted less than a week, Ward had a profound influence on Twain. The renowned comic recognized his Comstock colleague's talent, and he recommended that Twain leave the newspaper business, travel, write books, and give lectures, just as Ward himself was doing. He also offered to publish one of Twain's stories if the Comstock reporter could submit it in time for the release of *His Travels.* Twain failed to meet the deadline, but Ward arranged for the submission, a tale about a jumping frog in Calaveras County, California, to appear in *The Mercury,* a literary magazine published in New York. The story was an immediate success, launching Twain's national career as a fiction writer.

In 1865, Ward took his show to the South, where his act became one of the first efforts to heal the wounds after the Civil War: a Yankee comedian inspiring war-weary Southerners to laugh. Ward then set his sights on England, where he was, once again, a huge success. The strenuous trip proved too much for the performer, however. His health failed, and he died of tuberculosis in 1867 at the age of thirty-two.

Even before Ward vacated the stage, Twain began to follow in his mentor's footsteps, and circumstances had already inspired him to take much of Ward's advice when in the spring of 1864 Twain wrote an article that appeared in the *Territorial Enterprise,* suggesting that the women of the Sanitary Fund, the precursor to the American Red Cross, were using the money they were raising for a "Miscegenation Society," an imaginary organization that supposedly promoted interracial marriage. Twain insisted that he did not intend for the sketch to be published and that one of the *Territorial Enterprise* printers had used it against the author's wishes. Regardless, husbands of the defamed women were outraged, challenges to duels were exchanged, and Twain found it wise to slip out of the territory. But perhaps he was ready to leave anyway.

Twain relocated to California, where he began writing for a variety of outlets. Eventually, he won a commission to travel to the Hawaiian Islands as a correspondent for the *Sacramento Union.* The experience there and during a subsequent trip to the Holy Land provided the inspiration for writing books. In 1866 Twain began touring as a lecturer, typically posting advertisements that stated: "The doors open at 7:30; the trouble begins at 8:00." With that act, his career, combining witty writing, travel, and lectures, emulated that of Artemus Ward. Today, America remembers Twain while it has largely forgotten his trailblazing predecessor. Ward's approach to comedy consisted of one-liners shaped for the time, while Twain told imaginative, well-crafted stories that remain immortal.

It would be all too easy to end a discussion of the Comstock newspapers with Mark Twain, but the mining district's reporters amounted to much more than just this single career. Joe Goodman, the editor who hired Samuel Clemens, maintained his *Territorial Enterprise* as one of the finest expressions of journalism on the West Coast, setting a tone for the mining district through a decade of its most impressive production. Many Comstock writers experimented with fiction and tested the bounds of literature. Even Goodman's creativity was not constrained by the matter of publishing a paper. In 1871 he and a colleague, Rollin Mallory Daggett, wrote a play called *The Psychoscope.* A science fiction thriller, it was ahead of its time. Unfortunately for the authors, the realism it achieved in depicting the inner workings of a brothel was too much for Victorian-era sensibilities. After a few showings at Piper's Opera House, the play closed and drifted into obscurity. Nevertheless, *The Psychoscope* is another example of the intellectual vitality that the Comstock fostered. Daggett, Goodman's worthy co-author, went on to serve a term in Congress, followed by a stint as the U.S. minister to Hawaii. He then became a novelist and folklorist—achieving altogether the sort of diverse career that was typical of those who once worked in the field of Comstock journalism.

Goodman managed his newspaper until 1874 when William Sharon— a political opponent whom the newspaper publisher assailed during the 1872 U.S. Senate election—quietly purchased enough shares to oust the long-standing editor. Goodman took the proceeds of the sale, relocated to California, and began pursuing a new interest, a quest to decipher the Mayan calendar, and finally broke the code. The method he devised to understand the ancient script still bears his name, along with those of two other scholars. And he never lost touch with his old friend Mark Twain, with whom he continued a literary dialogue for decades. Goodman was in his late seventies when he died, in 1917. Lawrence Berkove, a respected scholar who has studied Goodman, Daggett, Clemens, and others, including Dan De Quille, has promoted the idea that these writers represented a distinct, remarkable contribution to American literature. Berkove calls this group the Sagebrush School, which he maintains is distinguished by its adherents' use of the Western tall tale and by their general irreverence.

While outrageous fiction was a hallmark of the region, some actual episodes of Comstock history seem as though they belong to a tall tale. In 1861 and 1864, the U.S. Army experimented with camels to bring salt and other goods from deep in the Great Basin back to the Comstock. Unfortunately, Great Basin terrain was too rocky. In addition, horses became skittish at the sight of camels, so the exotic beasts were allowed in Virginia City only after dark. Later, in 1875, the state legislature banned camels from public highways because they interfered with horse-drawn wagons. The test of various possibilities says more than the success or failure of the effort. The early Comstockers were inventive and open-minded. As a legacy, folklore insisted for decades that it was possible to see wild camels wandering in the Nevada hinterland.

As early as 1856, the U.S. Army experimented with the use of camels in the western North American deserts, but the animals failed to live up to expectations. In spite of this, entrepreneurs attempted to put them to use hauling supplies to Virginia City during the 1860s. (Courtesy of the Nevada Historical Society)

The master teller of tall tales, Mark Twain, returned to Virginia City in 1866 to lecture at Maguire's Opera House and then again in 1868, appearing at the same theater after John Piper purchased it. On his second and last visit to the Comstock, Twain attended the hanging of Jean Millian, a laundryman found guilty of strangling the courtesan Julia Bulette while she slept during the early-morning hours of January 20, 1867. The crime was one of the town's most notorious murders, lingering in the popular imagination well into the twentieth century when Bulette's biographers—and Virginia City in general—capitalized on the event. Bulette assumed superstar status through books, artwork, and a specially constructed gravesite visible through a telescope from the back of the Bucket of Blood Saloon on C Street.

Two years before Bulette's death, Virginia City brothel owner Jessie Lester met a similar fate. On Christmas night in 1864, Lester was shot as she tried to brace a door against an attacker. She languished for a month, suffering with the amputation of an arm. A devout Roman Catholic, she repented when death seemed imminent. The Daughters of Charity nursed her until she died, on January 23, 1865. She was buried in the consecrated ground of the Catholic cemetery but not before donating her estate to the Church. Lester had refused to identify her assailant, so unlike Julia Bulette, no folklore grew up around her, and her story faded from popular view.

And what of William Wright, Joe Goodman's star reporter? Dan De Quille, who preceded Mark Twain at the *Enterprise* and then served another thirty years after his departure, battled bouts of alcoholism throughout his life. Although he was widely regarded as the best author in the employment of the newspaper, the blockbuster that Twain seemed to write so easily eluded De Quille. With the publication of Twain's *Roughing It* in 1872, De Quille asked his friend for help with a sweeping history of the Comstock. His sojourn to Twain's house in Hartford, Connecticut, yielded mixed results, but as evidence that the old ties remained strong, Twain's publisher issued De Quille's masterwork, *The Big Bonanza* in 1876. While the book remains an excellent source for local history and offers moments of comic brilliance, it never became a best seller. Rather, De Quille's many fine, small pieces cause aficionados to regard him with admiration. In 1897, he returned to Iowa one last time, living on a pension quietly provided by John Mackay. He died there the following year in the embrace of his family. Wright remains a giant in the annals of Virginia City, although little more than a footnote on the national level.

The story of the Comstock is easily eclipsed by the brilliance of its mines and its technological achievements. These were extremely important, particularly during the early phase that established the district as one of the most famous centers of industry of all time. That having been said, the significance of the people who called Virginia City home, if only for a short period of time, adds a texture to the Comstock story that should never be underestimated or overlooked.

Chapter Three

The Big Bonanza

On May 14, 1863, miners working in the Ophir on the north end of the Comstock Lode broke into an excavation of the Burning Moscow. Two months earlier, the Ophir Mining Company had initiated a lawsuit against the Burning Moscow, asserting that its neighbor uphill to the west was cutting into the older Ophir claim, which dated back to the original 1859 strike. Ophir workers were following their vein of gold and silver and found that it was heading west. From the point of view of the owners of the Ophir, Burning Moscow miners were stealing Ophir ore by cutting down from the surface into Ophir property. According to the established rules of western mining camps, claimants had the right to follow a vein as it meandered underground through all its "dips and spurs." Ophir management insisted it was following its ore body as it drifted in the direction of the Burning Moscow, and the newer company maintained it was removing a discrete, separate ore body.

As workers from the two mines encountered one another on May 14, they formed into armed parties and engaged in an eerie underground battle. Burning Moscow forces repulsed those from the Ophir, the owners of which filed a complaint against their neighbors. The Territorial Supreme Court subsequently ordered the Burning Moscow to stop work until a judge had an opportunity to issue a ruling. But the fight was not over. The question about whether younger claims were pursuing separate ore bodies was to erupt into a district-wide debate that would affect the fate of the Comstock.

At the south end of Virginia City, the Chollar Mine and its younger neighbor, the Potosi, began a protracted legal contest over the same general issue: either the Comstock was composed of a single vein with legitimate claims crosscutting it along the north-south expanse of the deposit or there were many discrete deposits, allowing for claims extending to the east and west, up and down the hill. The ensuing debate lasted months, made a fortune for a future U.S. senator, played a role in the defeat of the first Nevada Constitution in January 1864, threatened the reelection of President Abraham Lincoln, and helped define mining law for the nation into the twenty-first century.

The Comstock became one of the world's best-known examples of the transition from placer mining to work underground. Perhaps it was inevitable, then, that the mining district also signaled a change away from gold seekers hoping to enjoy part of widespread successes. In the emerging reality, thousands of well-paid laborers helped make an elite few realize the dream of becoming millionaires. Two processes hastened and affected the unfolding of this new mining West.

First, there was the struggle to determine whether the gold and silver deposits were part of a single geological phenomenon or were separate and discrete from one another. The implication of this question was far-reaching. If the ore was distributed along a single fault that breached the surface and then descended deep underground, only claims along the north-south axis of the district were legitimate. The problem arose when a neighboring excavation uphill or downhill—to the west or east—of a primary claim began chasing ore. The owners with rights to the first claim of that area asserted that their neighbors were poaching from a single vein, while the counterargument was that there were many distinct, geologically unrelated pockets of gold and silver.

The consequence of the "single ledge" argument would be that fewer people would profit from Comstock wealth. If the ore was in fact a "multi-ledge" phenomenon, the chances of "striking it rich" would be greater for more people.

Initially, the Territorial Supreme Court took the side of the common man by ruling that there were multiple ledges of deposits in the district, distinct from one another. William Stewart, an emerging attorney representing wealthy single-ledge proponents, attempted an inspired political

William Stewart (1827–1909) played an important role in the legal battle over whether the Comstock Lode was a single geological structure or comprised numerous discrete ore bodies. With Nevada statehood in 1864, Stewart became a U.S. senator and helped establish the nation's approach to mining law. (Courtesy of the Nevada Historical Society)

solution by advocating the transformation of the Nevada territory into a state even though its population was far below the normally required one hundred thousand residents. In 1863 Abraham Lincoln coincidentally advanced the acceptance of Nevada into the Union because he feared he might lose the presidential contest the following year. Lincoln regarded the potential state of Nevada as supportive of his reelection and of the advancement of the Thirteenth Amendment to the U.S. Constitution, which abolished slavery.

Stewart saw an opportunity to exploit Lincoln's ambition because he recognized that the election of a new state supreme court could be controlled, placing sympathetic justices on the bench. In part as a reaction against Stewart and his single-ledge cause, a majority of the electorate was against a proposed state constitution in the January 1864 election. Opponents of Stewart's theory wanted to preserve the idea that multiple ledges existed and that virtually anyone could gain a share of the Comstock wealth, but as a consequence, they threatened to deprive the president of Nevada's electoral votes and supportive members of Congress who would assist with Lincoln's legislative agenda.

Fortunately for Lincoln and Stewart, mine productivity declined, causing a depression in late 1863 and into the next year. Many now believed that the court's support of multiple claims discouraged the corporate backing needed to probe ever deeper for elusive, profitable ore. Small private entrepreneurs were unable to assume the risk of extensive subterranean exploration. In addition, geologists determined that the Comstock gold and silver were deposited primarily along a single fault line. Mineralization occurred elsewhere in the area, inspiring hundreds of smaller operations, but the dream of striking rich ore bodies unrelated to the core Comstock fault system was becoming unrealistic. Only a few—those who held claims descended from the original owners of 1859—had the opportunity to win millions by retrieving underground ore.

Territorial judicial rulings reversed earlier opinions as the single-ledge argument won the day, but it was too late for those jurists who had crossed Stewart. With statehood achieved on October 31, 1864, a new slate of judges—handpicked by Stewart, who controlled the dominant Republican Party—assumed office. The most prominent of the displaced territorial judges left Nevada, never to return.

In the spring of 1865, while locked in yet another lawsuit, the Chollar and Potosi mines settled their differences and merged, ending the litigation that proximity seemed always to inspire. Stewart went on to become one of the two senators that Nevada first sent to Congress after statehood (the other one was territorial governor James Nye). Stewart occupied the seat from 1865 until 1875 and then returned to the U.S. Senate in 1887. He held that office until 1905, making him one of the longest-serving senators in Nevada history. President Lincoln, of course, won reelection in 1864. His margin was great enough that he did not need Nevada after all, which voted for him anyway. But the U.S. senators from the new state played an important role in passing the reconstruction and civil rights acts that Lincoln imagined before he was assassinated in 1865.

The second process that secured Comstock wealth for only the few also coincided with the downturn in the economy in 1864. A handful of investors, led by William Ralston, known as the man who built California, and clever William Sharon, gambled that there was still a lucrative future for the Comstock mines. Organizing as the Bank of California, they offered loans with low interest rates to distressed properties. Careful purchase of stocks gave the bank controlling interest of key claims. By directing scarce profitable ore away from financially troubled mills that were the very clients of his financial institution, Sharon could force his own customers into foreclosure.

Gaining possession of the foreclosed mills, the bank was able to establish a monopoly that controlled the industrial process, ranging from the procurement of supplies to underground excavation and the milling of ore. Stock manipulation became an easy prospect as Sharon moved profits from one end of the monopoly to another, perpetually selling stocks high only to devalue the business and purchase the shares back at a bargain. Unsuspecting investors, including everyone from local laborers to gentry in England, fell victim to practices that people a century later would regard as white-collar crime.

The Bank of California would have had a clear path to complete control of all that the Comstock could yield except that the salaried labor force would not accept unmitigated subjugation. In 1863 local workers organized the first miners' union west of the Mississippi. They demanded an increase in the daily wage from $3.50 per day to $4.00, but the effort was ill-timed. With the slump in the local economy, mine owners could claim that the demand of the miners' union was impractical and unrealistic. Because the appointed territorial governor, James Nye, owed nothing to a local electorate, he found it easy to side with the mine owners. He called out the federal troops from nearby Fort Churchill and crushed the union.

The miners learned a valuable lesson, however, and with statehood, they organized again and made certain that no one was elected to any significant office without expressing support for the workers. For the next twenty years, breaking a strike on the Comstock would be impossible, since the union had only to threaten to stop work to win whatever concession it wanted. A $4.00 daily wage became the standard. With the millions produced, it was a small concession for the bank and other owners to make in order to maintain peace and productivity. The legacy of this earliest of union struggles in the mines of the West has often been viewed as a chapter in labor history that was peaceful and resolved without conflict. In fact, the first phase of unionism was crucial. Miners quickly realized that the best way to handle management was to control its political environment to make certain that the rights—and salaries— of workers were always protected. And, of course, concessions were most easily secured when a union owned the apparatus of government with a solid, unassailable voting bloc.

The Comstock consequently became a balance between organized labor and corporate control of vast amounts of underground wealth. The single-ledge case and the Bank of California monopoly opened a new chapter for western mining history, and the power of the union defined how most workers would interact with the latest corporate reality. The Comstock and other hard-rock districts granted extraordinary rewards to a few people, leaving the rest to earn wages, albeit at better rates than in most occupations. But even these could be lost if the lure of the stock market proved too great. The pattern established by the California

Grafton T. Brown revisited Virginia City with a second bird's-eye view, published in 1864. The image depicted a growing community with many more substantial buildings than had existed in 1861. (Courtesy of Special Collections, University of Nevada-Reno Library)

Gold Rush of 1849, of widespread but limited wealth, became a distant, romanticized memory in the West.

One clear advantage of large corporate involvement was that big developments were now possible. The Bank of California used its profits to fund California and Bay Area infrastructure. Water projects opened on the East Bay. Among other ventures, the bank invested in ranches, farms, factories, the California wool industry, and the state's first winery. It built San Francisco's Palace Hotel, California Theatre, and New Montgomery Street. Perhaps the greatest achievement of the bank was the construction of the Virginia and Truckee Railroad, which, in

1872, linked the Comstock to the transcontinental railroad as it passed through Reno.

First of all, the laying of V&T track represented a remarkable feat of engineering. To ascend roughly 2,000 feet from Carson City to Virginia City, the surveyors found a path that caused the railroad to turn the equivalent of seventeen circles. Chinese immigrants—fresh from the completion of the transcontinental railroad—began hammering spikes to secure rail to wooden ties in 1869. Before the end of the year, locomotives traveled daily between Carson City and Gold Hill. Ore that teamsters formerly hauled by the wagonload was now transported in huge quantities at reduced prices. At the same time, critical supplies, including lumber needed underground, could arrive on the Comstock at much cheaper rates.

Mining depends on the value of the ore being greater than the cost of retrieval and milling. It is a business that works the margins. The Virginia and Truckee Railroad slashed the cost of supplies and transportation. Suddenly, poorer ore bodies that companies had previously ignored became profitable, extending the life of the mining district. Workers did not connect the V&T to Virginia City and the Reno link with the transcontinental railroad until 1872, but the effect of the shortline was obvious as early as 1869. Mills sprang up along the Carson River in areas too remote for wagons. And the mills in Washoe Valley, previously supplied by teamsters, died. The thriving towns of Ophir and Washoe City withered, the latter yielding its status of county seat in 1872 to the upstart community of Reno to the north.

The wealth of the Comstock allowed the V&T to purchase elegant steam engines and equipment. With nothing but the finest rolling on its rails and with the hauling of millions in ore and bullion, the railroad arguably became the most famous and profitable shortline in the world. Tourists sought the opportunity to ride across its spindly wooden Crown Point Trestle in Gold Hill, and the Virginia and Truckee became a household name throughout the nation.

One other by-product of the railroad was the 1869 construction of the U.S. Mint in Carson City, with its own private spur to deliver bullion to its door. Federal workers stamped tons of Comstock silver and gold into tens of thousands of coins from 1870 to 1893, each bearing the famed "CC" mint mark, one of the most coveted in the coin-collecting world.

It is not without irony that 1869, which saw the creation of a glamorous railroad and the opening of a U.S. Mint, was also a period of depression. The mines had exhausted the richest ore. Discouraged, people left for better prospects, and the abundant findings at Hamilton and Treasure Hill in eastern Nevada attracted many. But these were fly-by-night operations, resulting in a churning of the state's population as thousands came and went. Virginia City was home to some for only a few months. Others lingered, and those who returned from sojourns realized, eventually, that the Comstock could still yield wealth.

Organizing the technical and corporate infrastructure to exploit the ore beneath the ground was a critical step toward transforming the Comstock into a mining powerhouse. At the same time, the community had to manage itself and be content with the organic way it grew. Creating roads—both for wagons and for locomotives—required impressive feats of engineering. Equally remarkable was the development of hoist works, steam engines, and stamp mills, along with roiling vats used to separate bullion from waste. These achievements were at the core of the Virginia City story. More than that, the town was a magnet that attracted attention and, as a consequence, people. These new residents had lives to live, and they demanded all that the nineteenth century promised as the standard of civilization.

Almost immediately, the Comstock was faced with the threat of fire, but without established fire companies, residents were too often defenseless. In early 1861, Tom Peasley, a New Yorker with some background in firefighting, organized what may have been the first of its kind in town, the Virginia Engine Company #1. Several others followed, but the enthusiasm of these voluntary efforts at times exceeded their effectiveness. Fire destroyed buildings and sometimes whole blocks throughout the 1860s and early 1870s. It is easy to imagine that the devastation would have been far worse had Peasley and his volunteers not done what they could to fight back.

Peasley, who had made his living in the saloon business, died in a Carson City bar brawl on February 2, 1866. Martin V. Barnhart, a twenty-three-year-old native of Indiana, was a member of a Carson City fire department. He had a grudge against Peasley, and he shot him without provocation. Peasley fought back, and although Barnhart managed to break the handle of his pistol over Peasley's skull, the Virginia City fire chief refused to succumb before firing the last shot in the disagreement, killing Barnhart on the spot. That done, Peasley asked that his boots be removed and that someone send for his brother. Thus passed one of the favorites of the Comstock during its first decade.

Peasley's life and then his death had ramifications for the story of Julia Bulette, the prostitute who figured in the previous chapter. Thanks to his sponsorship, Bulette became an honorary member of Engine Company #1. A photo—perhaps commemorating the occasion—is the only known image of the Comstock's legendary courtesan. She had been a favorite of Peasley's. Now, with his murder, Bulette found herself with failing health and no patron. As it turned out, she had less than a year to live. People like Peasley and Bulette came and went in the midst of the outstanding growth of the mining district, lives lived and sometimes tragically ended as the larger story unfolded.

Besides fire companies, much was necessary to organize a real community. Virginia City incorporated in 1861 under Utah Territory. Later that year it became the seat of government for Storey County within Nevada Territory. The community now hosted both county and city government, complete with a distinct sheriff's office and police department, courts, jails, and the various other public offices needed to run local government.

Thanks to a remarkable collection of records preserved in the Storey County Courthouse, it is possible to peer into this early period of growth to see how property was exchanged and businesses formed. While mining was the focus of the district, a host of other businesses sprang up to address the tastes of the residents. Because Virginia City and Gold Hill were a day's ride from the closest communities and several days removed from any place with substantial shopping, all necessities had to be furnished locally. Money was no object in a place that was yielding millions, so local establishments could afford to import whatever people wanted from the international marketplace. A wide variety of stores offering everything from hardware and groceries to tobacco products, clothing, books, and toys came to dominate Virginia City's central commercial corridor. Gold Hill was a smaller town that served mainly as a place for workers to live. Although it too had many businesses, including banks, restaurants, and saloons, Gold Hill's growth was stunted by its proximity to Virginia City, which drew on the entire area for customers.

Living in an urban center, most people did not need to own a horse, and many could not afford the expense, but the period nevertheless relied heavily on these animals as a source of labor and transportation. Therefore, the community supported a full range of livery stables, wagon and carriage shops, and blacksmiths. Because health is always an issue, there were doctors, dentists, and drugstores. A transitory population demanded hotels, and when some people wanted to linger, they required lodging houses and boardinghouses, the latter offering meals as well as a place to sleep. For those seeking a more permanent domicile, a range of tradesmen—carpenters, plumbers, painters, glaziers, sash makers and the like—were prepared to build houses. Restaurants of all kinds, reflecting numerous ethnicities, offered a full assortment of possibilities. Because some businesses were destined to fail or simply because people were constantly on the move, auctioneers assisted in the sale of property. And when transactions did not unfold according to expectations, an army of lawyers was available to offer assistance.

And none of this even touches on the subject of alcohol. At its height, Virginia City boasted having one hundred saloons, but that statistic alone does nothing to shed light on the nature of the institution. Dozens of these businesses could not survive if they were in direct competition with one another. Saloon owners did everything they could to create a niche that would allow them to thrive. Most failed after only a few months or a year or two, but a few became long-lasting institutions. Nevertheless, the incentive was there to make each place a little different from the others.

The most obvious way saloons distinguished themselves from one another was in the price that the barkeeper charged and the quality that it implied. Virginia City had one-bit and two-bit saloons, the former charging twelve and a half cents for a beer, a whiskey, or a cigar, and the latter assessing a quarter of a dollar for each of these indulgences. Only a handful of the town's saloons were of the two-bit variety, places reserved for the wealthy who were willing to pay a price to drink exclusively with the elite. Most Comstock saloons were one-bit establishments, and these covered a wide range in terms of quality. Some, such as Piper's Old Corner Bar, offered a refined presentation for the bargain price, while others were little more than the crudest of settings.

Cost was not the only way to differentiate businesses. One saloon would offer billiards, while a neighbor might be known for a specific type of food. Patrons could have a haircut at one, and another would offer current newspapers. Some saloons attempted to earn notoriety by providing a remarkable spread of fixings for a free lunch, presumably after a purchased drink.

One means of entertainment that seems strange to the modern world was shooting galleries within saloons. A handful of these institutions allowed patrons to drink and take target practice at the same time. Since the buildings were usually long and narrow, the target would naturally be at the back end of the saloon, the shooter near the front, and a row of patrons would face the bar as bullets whizzed past their backs. An archaeological excavation of one of these sites revealed that many of the cartridges were "stubbies," meaning that they were short and contained very little powder. Nevertheless, at least one newspaper article reported on a death, in this case an adolescent boy who was paid to set up new targets, but who did not step out of the way in time to avoid the patron's shot.

Many saloons catered to specific ethnic groups. William A. G. Brown opened the Boston Saloon during the Civil War to serve African Americans. The business lasted for nearly a dozen years, although it moved once, and a newspaper article dating to 1866 indicates that a French immigrant was patronizing the establishment. Similarly, saloons with French, German, or Italian monikers did not necessarily mean that only immigrants from those nations were welcomed. Still, by employing a certain name and celebrating the heritage of a specific group in advertisements, various saloons sought to attract part of the market. Shanahan and O'Connor's Hibernia Brewery and Saloon may have welcomed people of diverse backgrounds, but it was clearly Irish, and one can imagine that those who opposed nationalism for the Emerald Isle would have found a chilly reception there.

Businesses with names utilizing the term "brewery" have left later residents to believe that these establishments actually brewed beer. That was not always the case. A saloon could claim to be a brewery if it had a contract with a place where beer was brewed. The term meant that the saloon offered beer on tap, not just by the bottle. In 1987, Virginia City's Union Brewery petitioned the state legislature for permission to open a microbrewery in its establishment. Restrictions were tight before the craze for microbreweries swept the nation. After much deliberation, Nevada lawmakers decided to allow limited brewing of beer in locations that had traditionally done this in the past. The Union probably never made its own beer during the nineteenth century, but with the law changed, it offered home-brewed beer into the 1990s.

As expressed through the names of its saloons—and restaurants, for that matter—one of the hallmarks of the Comstock was its international population. The 1860 census captured growing but rather simple towns where the vast majority of the residents were men and most called themselves miners. Ten years later, the mining district had grown in diversity and numbers: more than 11,300 people were documented in Storey County. There were many more women than before, although at 2,237, they represented no more than a quarter of the adults. With the establishment of families, there was a sizable increase in the number of children: 2,467—or almost a quarter of the population—were sixteen years old or younger.

By 1870, the number of different occupations had swelled by the hundreds. There were roughly 2,600 miners, representing 40 percent of the adult men. Miners were still a significant bloc, but now carpenters, cooks, engineers, teamsters, and merchants made up an ever-larger part of the community.

Over 70 percent of the women in 1870—more than 1,600—were recorded with "keeping house" as an occupation. This vague term offers little information as to what each woman was actually doing. Mary McNair Mathews was a widowed mother who called Virginia City her home during the period and later published an account of her Comstock sojourn. In her *Ten Years in Nevada,* Mathews described herself as pursuing six different occupations, among them teaching at home, washing clothes, maintaining boarders, and plying the needle trades. Yet Victorian-era propriety led most in her situation to claim the generic "keeping house." In Mathews's case, her profession remained blank in the 1870 census. When the census enumerator did record an occupation for women that year, nearly two hundred were identified as prostitutes, using one term or another. Even assuming that many of those involved in sexual commerce misled the census enumerator, there is no reason to believe that their number ever exceeded 8 percent of the adult women, the majority of whom led respectable lives throughout the history of the Comstock. For the few who actually claimed an occupation other than keeping house, those working with garment or hat production or mending were the largest group. Others, including servants, cooks, clerks, and teachers, joined the ranks of an increasingly complex society.

One of the most impressive characteristics of the Comstock by 1870, however, was the number of immigrants. As Twain would remark in *Roughing It,* his fictionalized account of his Comstock sojourn, "all the peoples of the earth had representative adventurers in the Silverland." The international nature of the community would have been startling for many who arrived from eastern states and came to make up the other half of Virginia City. While there were immigrants from every inhabited continent, some places dominated: Ireland contributed more to the mining district than any other place. England—with most from Cornwall— came in as a close second; there were also hundreds from China, Canada, and Germany. Although the Chinese formed a distinct Chinatown several blocks below the commercial corridor, many of their numbers were scattered about Virginia City, working as laundrymen, servants, and cooks. Other nations also added to the exotic diversity, and yet those from Australia, New Zealand, France, Italy, Russia, Turkey, Morocco, the Isle of Man, and dozens of other places were too few to form distinct communities.

The local Spanish-speaking population rarely exceeded one hundred throughout the history of the Comstock, and its nature changed through time. While at first most were from California or Mexico, this part of the district eventually came to include more Chileans. Other people from North America usually arrived from states such as New York, Ohio, Pennsylvania, and Massachusetts. The majority of young people were born in California or Nevada, but they could look to their parents for their own distinct ethnic identities. Most African Americans—who also never numbered more than one hundred—came largely from southern or border states and were apparently recently-emancipated slaves. Whether few or numerous, the immigrants from the various nations made the Comstock a complex place. This was the nature of Comstock society after the population stabilized in the wake of a slump in mine productivity in 1869.

That year also witnessed the worst industrial accident in Comstock history and the beginning of yet another of its remarkable engineering feats. On the morning of April 7, a fire that had been smoldering at the 800-foot level of the Yellow Jacket Mine, just above the present-day Gold Hill Hotel, caused the timbers to finally collapse. The force of the resulting cave-in sent a torrent of poisonous air rushing throughout the mine and into the neighboring Kentuck and Crown Point excavations. The disaster occurred just as the morning shift was reporting for duty, but fortunately not everyone was underground for the day yet; otherwise the death toll would have been much higher. As it was, at least thirty-five

The Comstock's most famous mining accident occurred on April 7, 1869, when a fire started at the 800-foot level of the Yellow Jacket Mine in Gold Hill. Poisonous gases and smoke permeated the Yellow Jacket and then flooded into the neighboring Kentuck and Crown Point Mines. At least thirty-five miners perished. Many could not be recovered. (Courtesy of the authors)

men lost their lives. The exact count is unknown because the heat of the blaze hindered efforts to retrieve the remains from every part of the mine.

The disaster sent a shudder through the Comstock workforce. Incidents of death and injury were inevitable when working with heavy equipment underground and when dealing with shafts and explosives. But the death of thirty-five fellow miners in one catastrophe was unprecedented. Adolph Sutro, the entrepreneur who had previously advocated a long drainage tunnel, stepped forward, pointing a finger of blame and suggesting a solution. This time, people listened.

As previously noted, Sutro had advocated for a tunnel that would extend from the Carson River Valley near Dayton to the Comstock mines, intersecting at the 1,640-foot level. Although he organized his company in 1865 and was greeted with initial support, the Comstock leadership—and especially the Bank of California management—recognized that Sutro's plan would place him in extraordinary control of all profits. His tunnel would provide the cheapest way to enter and leave the mine, so workers would naturally want to live in his town, which was platted under the name Sutro. The least expensive way to deliver ore to a mill, coincidentally owned by Sutro, would also be through the tunnel, so he would control the profits associated with producing bullion while charging a fee for everything that would exit his tunnel. And the same would be true of water; while his tunnel would lower the cost of pumping, Sutro would be able to charge the mines for dewatering the underground works. In other words, Sutro's tunnel would place him in a powerful position to control the Comstock, and initial resistance to his proposal stopped him from beginning his project.

The Yellow Jacket disaster provided Sutro with an opportunity. He pointed to the Comstock power brokers and alleged that they had prevented the excavation of his tunnel, which would have provided a means of escape for the victims, saving dozens of lives. His argument was certainly flawed, since most of the miners did not die for want of an exit at a lower level, but Sutro did manage to strike an emotional chord. The Bank of California and the other owners of Comstock mines now saw fewer reasons to oppose Sutro's proposal. The district was in a slump, and it might not survive to see Sutro actually begin his enormous undertaking.

And besides, with the Virginia and Truckee Railroad delivering ore to new mills along the Carson River, the incentive to patronize Sutro's tunnel diminished. Undaunted, he began raising funds for his venture.

Sutro began work on October 19, 1869. With 20,489 feet—more than three miles—of excavation ahead of them, his workers faced countless months of labor before the business would produce any profits. In order to achieve the desired results, the tunnel would require twice the width of a normal mine, allowing for carts to travel back and forth simultaneously. In addition, the excavation would need to rise at a steady slow rate so it would intersect with the mines at the lowest possible point, and it could not have dips that would fill with water. Engineers consequently devised a system using a surveying station above the tunnel's entrance that reflected sunlight every day at noon back into the tunnel from a corresponding station near the tunnel entrance. That way, the sun would provide the means to guarantee that the tunnel never strayed from its course and trajectory.

On September 1, 1878, after nearly nine years of labor, Sutro's workers broke into the Savage Mine. The engineering was so precise that the opening deviated only eighteen inches from the original plan. Because of a difference in elevation between the mine and the tunnel entrance, the opening caused a strong wind to howl until pressure equalized. Excitement was immediate. Begun during a slump on the Comstock, the tunnel was completed as fortunes seemed once again to fade. Sutro's project held the promise of lowering costs and making the Comstock profitable for many more years. Stock in his corporation rose, but apparently Sutro recognized that his endeavor would never meet expectations. He cashed in his interests and relocated to San Francisco as a newly minted millionaire, then went on to acquire vast areas of real estate in his adopted city. He developed the Cliff House, and founded the nearby Sutro Baths and Sutro Library. He served as mayor from 1895 to 1897, then died the following year at sixty-eight.

The Sutro Tunnel was given a minor royalty from the mines, which found it profitable to pump no higher than the 1,600-foot level. Had the royalty exceeded the expense of pumping to the surface, the mine owners would have bypassed the tunnel. In addition, mills along the river elsewhere did, in fact, command the market, so there was no chance that the new tunnel would inspire any company to abandon the existing infrastructure. Although much of the Sutro's work collapsed by the mid-twentieth century, it still passively drains the Comstock mines at the 1,600-foot level. Water continues to exit from the tunnel entrance every hour of every day.

In spite of short-term downturns in the profitability of various mines in 1863 and 1869, the strength of the Comstock was in its ability to sustain itself until the discovery of the next bonanza, and the investment in the infrastructure made survival possible. For twenty years, whenever there seemed to be no more viable ore bodies to be discovered, mine production would improve and those who stuck with the Comstock found their patience rewarded. Still, only a remarkable optimist during the 1869 depression would have anticipated what was right around the corner—the discovery of what came to be known as the Big Bonanza.

John Mackay, the humble Irishman who arrived in Virginia City in 1859 without a cent, had begun work as a wage earner while retaining the dream of something bigger. Like many, he speculated on what were apparently worthless mining claims because they could be purchased for little money. In 1866 Mackay and a partner acquired a Gold Hill mine called the Kentuck, which he began to work with little more than his own two hands and the strength of his back.

Irish native John Mackay (1831–1902) arrived on the Comstock in 1859. With hard work and shrewd investments, he became a famed silver baron and one of the richest men in the world. (Courtesy of the Nevada Historical Society)

Similar to other wage earners who tested their luck at pursuing their own excavations, Mackay used the crudest, cheapest technology possible. He sank a shaft, gaining access with a hand winch while his more affluent, modern neighbors used steam power to hoist men and ore from the depths. Nevertheless, Mackay's efforts paid off. He discovered a small bonanza and managed to reach millionaire status. He was not the richest or the most notable Comstocker at the time, but he had achieved something significant. While that could have been the end of the story, a more extraordinary chapter was about to unfold.

James Fair, another Irish immigrant who had arrived on the Comstock in the early 1860s, was to play a pivotal role in the next act of Virginia City's drama. He came with experience and quickly found employment as a supervisor, assuming control of the Ophir Mine in 1865. He then became superintendent of the Hale and Norcross Mine two years later. After a year, the owners dismissed Fair for reasons that remain murky, but clearly he was gathering knowledge about the Comstock that would help him later.

Eventually Mackay and Fair met and realized that a partnership would benefit them both. In 1869, they increased their chances of winning Comstock riches when they contacted James C. Flood and William S. O'Brien, affluent San Francisco saloonkeepers turned stockbrokers. Mackay and Fair approached their fellow Irishmen with the idea of forming a joint venture to pursue the purchase of the Hale and Norcross. After maneuvering to acquire a controlling interest in the property, the partners elected their own officers and began the steady acquisition of other mines. For good measure, they purchased ore processing mills to protect their profits from being manipulated by William Sharon and the Bank Crowd.

The Bank of California had a stranglehold on the Comstock, and it must have seemed that the monopoly could not be broken. But William Sharon had made a series of costly errors in misguided attempts to gain control of all Comstock industrial operations for the bank. A fatal flaw in the institution's armor was revealed in 1871 when one of its investors, Alvinza Hayward, conspired with his brother-in-law, John P. Jones, to make a grab for the Crown Point Mine in Gold Hill. Jones was the superintendent of the mine, and he realized that there was profitable ore available and that the Crown Point's stock was undervalued. The two quietly cornered the market on the mine's public holding, and before Sharon knew what had happened, his opponents seized control. Stunned, Sharon offered a deal to Jones and Hayward that resulted in a trade. The bank sold the rest of its Crown Point stock to the two men. They, in turn, sold their interest in the neighboring Belcher Mine of Gold Hill. The settlement hardly brought peace, however: Jones continued to be a thorn in Sharon's side, defeating the latter the following year in a bid to represent Nevada in the U.S. Senate.

Whether because he was weakened or distracted, Sharon failed to notice when Mackay, Fair, Flood, and O'Brien focused their attentions on Virginia City's Best and Belcher Mine. The slice of claim had failed to be profitable, but Fair and Mackay speculated that something big slumbered in the depths. When the value of the Best and Belcher's stock plummeted in 1871, the four Irishmen snatched up shares at bargain prices. Their new acquisition, and especially their move into the neighboring ConVirginia Mine, would become part of international mining lore.

As he pursued underground exploration, Fair recognized a slip of mineralization, which he followed into the depths at the 1,200-foot level. At times, as the tale goes, the trail nearly disappeared, but Fair had the prospecting instincts of a bloodhound, and he directed the miners where to dig. Throughout the autumn of 1873, the vein grew stronger, and then it finally unfolded into what early Comstock historian Eliot Lord compared with a renowned story from *Arabian Nights:* "The plain facts are as marvellous as a Persian Tale, for the young Aladdin did not see in the glittering case of the genii such fabulous riches as were lying in the dark womb of rock." The discovery, forever known as the "Big Bonanza," fueled an economic boom that lasted for several years. With the resulting flush times, the Comstock reached its largest size with perhaps as many as 25,000 people living in Virginia City and Gold Hill.

The discovery of the Big Bonanza made Mackay and Fair two of the richest men in the world, and they were consequently able to leverage any number of projects or fulfill whatever personal ambitions they might have. The Bonanza Firm quickly formed the Nevada Bank of San Francisco to challenge the primacy of the Bank of California, causing the older institution to falter. With incredible wealth at their disposal, Fair used his profits to purchase a seat in the U.S. Senate, becoming notable as one of the most ineffective members in the history of that august body. Mackay remained a hardworking miner, but he later invested in the laying of telegraph cables across the Atlantic and Pacific Oceans.

Mackay and Fair, together with their wives, ultimately played leading roles in something of a morality play, answering the question about how sudden wealth can affect people. Mackay, the humble and genuinely admirable man, remained unchanged, becoming known locally for his quiet philanthropy and general kindness. Marie Louise Mackay used the fortune to establish herself in European and New York society as a fixture of the aristocracy. Comstockers saw her as someone who was pretentious, abandoning her husband for the high life a continent and an ocean away. Although the Mackays remained close by all accounts, public perception caused judgment to fall against the woman who lived life large while her husband ventured underground nearly every day to inspect the property that gave her the wealth she enjoyed. Fair, who was regarded as a shrewd businessman with a dark heart, had a failed marriage and an increasing reputation for being disagreeable. Theresa Fair was beloved for her generosity, but she became the suffering wife, eventually divorcing her husband for habitual philandering.

At the same time that the Big Bonanza was about to infuse a spectacular amount of wealth into Virginia City and the American West, a feat of engineering unfolded that remains as one of the Comstock's most remarkable achievements. Since the first strikes in 1859, people had complained about the quality of the water in the mining district. The local supplier provided what locals called "the best of tunnel water," pumped from mines with the least contamination of minerals and toxins. In 1871—two years before the discovery of the Big Bonanza—John Mackay, James Fair, and some other investors settled on a plan to remedy the situation. That year, they purchased the Virginia City Water Company from William Sharon. The new owners of the company hired Hermann Schussler, a German who was educated at the Prussian Military Academy at Oldenburg. He also studied and worked in engineering in Switzerland. After immigrating to the United States in 1864, Schussler helped design the Spring Valley Water Works for the San Francisco Bay Area. This was followed by additional work throughout the region, each undertaking increasing his knowledge and his reputation for being able to build ambitious water projects. When he arrived on the Comstock, he was faced with a daunting task as well as an opportunity to create his most extraordinary system.

Virginia City's situation presented a formidable challenge. The nearest source of good water was the Sierra Nevada Range several miles to the west, and a deep valley separated it from Virginia City. Schussler arrived at a solution that consisted of dams to capture water from creeks feeding into Lake Tahoe, nestled within the Sierra. From there, flumes led to a tunnel that fed a reservoir on the east slope of the mountain range. This, in turn, filled a pipe that dropped to the south end of Washoe Valley and with the pressure of that descent, forced the water back up to a point above Virginia City. There, the water flowed into yet another reservoir, which served a system of pipes that transported it to the various Comstock communities. Beginning some 8,000 feet above sea level, the entire system relied on gravity rather than expensive pumping.

Risdon Iron Works in San Francisco provided the seven hundred tons of iron pipe. This, together with its 1,524 lead-sealed joints, had to withstand a maximum of 1,200 column feet of water pressure, the equivalent of 800 pounds per square inch at its lowest point. Transforming Schussler's vision into reality was no easy task; forging and assembling this material challenged the limits of Victorian-era technology. Nevertheless, in the summer of 1873, Schussler's system of flumes, tunnels, reservoirs, and pipes began to deliver water. In honor of the event, the National Guard fired "General Grant," the cannon at Fort Homestead above Gold Hill. The fact that the community still uses the system—even though the state eventually replaced all the pipes and lead-filled joints— is testimony to the brilliance of Schussler's design. The engineer went on to develop Nevada water projects in Pioche and Tuscarora and as far away as Hawaii. Hermann Schussler died in 1919 in San Francisco.

During the dynamic period of the early 1870s, Senator William Stewart, champion of the single-ledge theory, secured a legacy on the national stage with his work in Congress. Upon arriving in 1865, he turned his attention to crafting railroad legislation, but his previous experience with mining regulations and litigation quickly won him a spot on the Senate Committee on Mines and Mining. Once in the U.S. Senate, Stewart maneuvered with legislative skill to protect the interests of mining, amending a bill called "An Act granting the Right of Way to Ditch and Canal Owners over the Public Lands, and for other Purposes." Popularly known in the industry as the Mining Act of 1866, Stewart's addition to the bill granted miners free access to mineral deposits on public lands. The act also addressed the thorny issue of patenting lode claims, giving mining districts authority based on local customs and what the California State Legislature had approved in 1851. After decades of debate and expensive court battles about mineral exploration on public lands, miners now worked within a legal structure. An amendment in 1870 allowed placer miners to purchase, with proof, the claims they had diligently worked.

Stewart subsequently outmaneuvered his opponents in the Senate to help pass the National Mining Act of 1872, which outlined the specific records that miners needed in order to support a legitimate claim as well as how to maintain their claims from year to year. It also required mining districts to comply with federal standards when drafting local laws. The 1872 act was controversial from the start, but it survives as the bedrock of national mining policy into the twentieth-first century. Stewart's prominent role in crafting legislation on railroads, irrigation, and mining along with his advocacy for the cause of silver as a standard for the currency allowed him to bolster his national reputation while affecting Nevada politics to the present. Senator Stewart died in 1909 at the age of eighty-one.

With the discovery of the Big Bonanza in 1873, the great Comstock Lode gained a degree of fame in the mining world that grants it a lasting place in history. Wealth poured into the community and caused San Francisco to glow more brightly than ever. The sudden influx of silver onto the market shook the world's economy, inspiring governments to question linking currency to the precious metal. The months after the 1873 strike created a time of remarkable affluence, and for those who lived and worked in Virginia City and neighboring Gold Hill, it must have seemed that the good times could not end.

Chapter Four

Disaster and Rebirth

During the night of October 25, 1875, the wind howled. Those familiar with Virginia City and its famed Washoe Zephyrs had experienced this before. It had been a dry summer, and many might have looked at the unsettled night as a sign that rain or snow was on its way. Indeed, it was a harbinger of the first winter storm. But the wind would come to represent something much more than that.

At five thirty the next morning, before the sun rose on October 26, a drunk miner returned to his room at "Crazy Kate" Shea's boardinghouse on A Street. He lit a kerosene lamp and knocked it over, starting a blaze that soon engulfed his room and the entire boardinghouse. With the structure fully consumed, the wind began its work, rushing the flames from building to building and block to block.

As a means of conserving water, the Virginia City Water Company regularly turned off its system in the early morning hours. Consequently, the first firefighters to arrive on the scene went to fire hydrants and found them dry. Some frantically tried to rouse an official from the company to charge the system while others used whatever they could to battle the flames. There was little that could be done. Property owners desperately moved furniture and other possessions away from the raging fire, placing them in streets that seemed out of danger, only to see the disaster outpace them and incinerate what they thought they had saved.

The 1875 bird's-eye view of Virginia City featured the community as it appeared before the fire that occurred later that year. It documents a town that was grand but retained some of the more primitive buildings of its beginnings. Virginia City rebuilt itself into an opulent expression of the wealth of the 1870s. (Courtesy of the Library of Congress, 76693079)

The inferno roared downhill ahead of the wind and at the same time crept uphill and to the north and south. Hundreds of structures fell to the flames. Witnesses described fire tornados swirling into the air as the monster produced its own weather system in its search for fuel and oxygen. Piper's Opera House, the building Maguire had opened in July of 1863, succumbed to dynamite as firefighters struggled to create a wall of debris to stop the onslaught. Their efforts failed; the fire devoured the structure on the ground just as it would have had it been standing.

From as far away as Fort Churchill, twenty miles to the southeast, people could see the rising plume of smoke in the direction of Virginia City. One person wrote in a letter that during the day, charred pages of hymnals, carried by the wind, fluttered down from above. Even at that distance, it was clear that something horrible was happening.

Regardless of which church's hymnbooks were being tossed into the air by the fire, much has been made about the story of yet another dynamiting. Comstock folklore includes a tale about John Mackay directing his miners to set charges to blow up the Catholic church. According to the legend, Father Patrick Manogue tried to stop Mackay, insisting that it would be blasphemy to destroy the sacred edifice. Mackay responded that if he could save the mines, he would have the money to build a new church. Many in the community discount the story, perhaps regarding the purposeful destruction of St. Mary in the Mountains as inconceivable. Still, dynamiting buildings to throw obstacles in the way of a rampaging fire was a common strategy in the nineteenth century.

The tactic was particularly appropriate on October 26 because a fierce wind would fling flaming debris from a tall building, or in this case a tall steeple, throwing it far away to ignite additional fires. And there was a real danger that if the pump houses for the mines burned, the underground would flood, damaging the works. Such a calamity would cut off the avenues for further exploration at a time when no viable new bodies of ore had been located. According to the legend, Mackay believed that if the aboveground equipment were destroyed, it would be impossible to justify the expense of dewatering the excavations and rebuilding the mine supports to resume exploration. Virginia City's industrial economy could be destroyed by the fire, ending the lifeblood of the community. The idea that the church was dynamited as a firebreak is not only possible but completely plausible.

Despite the intensity of the inferno, only three fatalities occurred. Passersby pleaded with a man in the Ash Book and Toy Store to leave the doomed structure. Undaunted, and seemingly drunk, he responded by hurling toys at the frantic spectators until the building collapsed on him. A crumbling wall of the Carson Brewery claimed another man as he hurried to escape the flames, and cleanup crews retrieved the skeletal remains of a third victim who was never identified. In all, the catastrophe claimed few lives relative to the destruction it left behind.

When the fire had burnt itself out and all that remained was smoldering debris in a broad swath through the center of town, the temperature fell and a snowstorm set in. The state militia stayed on duty during the night to prevent looting and to restore order to the devastated streets of Virginia City, but given the sudden turn in the weather, there was probably little need. Witnesses estimated that ten thousand homeless residents camped on the hillside, although there is also ample testimony of those whose houses survived opening their doors to refugees. During the night, two feet of snow accumulated in Virginia City, a blessing in the sense that it extinguished all that remained of the flames, although it posed a challenge for those exposed to the elements.

The disaster was a shock to the region. San Francisco and its Bay Area had depended on Comstock wealth to bolster the region's own affluence, and many were invested in mining company stocks. Perhaps more to the point, countless people had traveled to Virginia City or knew those who lived there at one time or another. The Nevada and California communities were entwined financially, socially, and culturally. The response to the fire was direct and significant. When word got out that Virginia City was in dire need of blankets, clothing, furniture, and lumber, towns in both states pitched in with cash donations for the homeless and supplies for rebuilding.

What Virginia City did not receive as contributions, it quickly purchased: the firefighters and the frantic efforts of others, including John Mackay, could not save the commercial center of town, but the mines had survived for the most part. With gold and silver bullion still in production, the affluence of the community made rebuilding that much easier. The schedule of the Virginia and Truckee Railroad expanded to the maximum capacity of track and available engines. Contemporaries describe up to fifty trains arriving each day, hauling supplies including the material needed to rebuild. Virginia City rose from the ashes better than ever. The post-fire community was ostentatious, displaying its legendary wealth for everyone—especially investors—to see.

While the capital of western mining had every reason to be hopeful, more importantly, it had to appear optimistic. Stockholders were wary immediately after the fire. They watched for a sign that it was time to quit the Comstock. Indeed, many of the Chinese did leave, perhaps suspicious that there was little reason to invest in rebuilding and concerned that the post-fire confidence was little more than bravado. Nevertheless, even in Chinatown there was reconstruction. Those who remained in Virginia City, regardless of place of birth, believed there was every motivation to rebuild.

So it began, and what occurred left posterity with much of what one sees today. No expense was spared, and the local newspapers declared victory with each new facade that was erected and with every new building that opened for business. Because construction occurred so rapidly, there is a homogeneity in the commercial blocks of the fire zone. The railroad imported building components that were quickly assembled into dozens of establishments, and although they were not all produced by the same California entrepreneurs, it is evident that they belong to the same moment in history. Regardless of appearance, each structure exhibits the pride of the period when the Comstock proved its vitality. No more is this true than for the public buildings, the courthouse, and the churches of Virginia City.

The humble Presbyterian church of the 1860s survived, standing far enough to the south that it escaped the fire's path. The three other major churches were destroyed that day, and the Episcopalian, Methodist, and Catholic congregations were forced to rebuild. The Episcopalians, perhaps never more than one hundred in number, did not need a large church. As many of their members came from the more affluent ranks of the community, funding the rebuilding effort was relatively easy. The result is St. Paul's, a charming Gothic Revival wooden edifice with a steep gable and spire, but its interior is what is most captivating about the structure. Soaring rafters and wall boards installed diagonally lift the eyes. Because the lumber is varnished rather than painted, the interior glows with golden brown hues. The original large organ, its steel-gray pipes and wooden sound boxes reaching to a point where they nearly touch the ceiling, dominates a front corner of the sanctuary to the side of the altar. In all, the Episcopalian place of worship boasts one of the

Comstock's more elegant interiors, noted for its combination of simplicity and grace.

The rebuilt Methodist church, home to the Cornish population and the rare person with Welsh roots, also relied on wood. Unlike the willowy Gothic architecture of the Episcopal church, the Methodists built a place with a substantial, blocklike tower. The structure spoke of strength and substance more than elegance. Unfortunately, the building is no longer extant, so it is not possible to describe its interior. The fact that it is the only major church to have vanished from the Virginia City landscape is tied directly to its history: the Cornish immigrants were the first to leave when the mines failed. They were so thoroughly immersed in the mining industry that they were constantly prepared to move to the next bonanza. Years later, with the bulk of its congregation gone, the church itself left the Comstock: in 1913 Methodists moved it to Sparks, Nevada, where it served another congregation until 1956. Baptists then purchased the real estate, but tore down the building the following year.

The Catholic church was the most impressive of the four major churches in Virginia City. This should not be surprising, since it was the spiritual home for more than a third of the community, including the dominant neighborhoods of Irish immigrants and their children. Father Manogue, who came to play a pivotal role in the Virginia City parish, erected churches after his arrival in 1862 and again in 1868. After the fire, for a third time, he set to work. Perhaps Manogue's exchange with Mackay during the fire was apocryphal. The silver baron was known for his generosity, but his contribution was not the only source for financing the reconstruction. Newspapers reported on fund-raising events hosted by the women of the congregation. Eager to rebuild their place of worship, they competed in assembling tables that enticed visitors to purchase a wide variety of products ranging from baked goods to fine handmade lace and letters scented with perfume that would profess to the bearer that he held a special place in the heart of the author.

It is impossible to unravel how effective these efforts were or how much the various sources actually donated. Undoubtedly, the resulting church is an awe-inspiring masterpiece of architecture. Constructed on the foundation and lower walls of the 1868 church, the new building exhibited Gothic details crafted in stone and wood that are more elaborate than those of its predecessor. With the tip of its spire reaching 133½ feet, the edifice became one of the most visible in the community, and it remains arguably the most photographed historic structure in the state. Complementing its appearance, the spire is home to a bell that weighs more than a ton, with a hundred-pound clapper. The interior is no less impressive: redwood columns and intricately carved Gothic rafters support a soaring blue ceiling. Maria Theresa Fair, drawing on the fortune secured by her husband, James Fair, donated a large ornate zinc baptistery. Above a Gothic altar is a painting of a pregnant Virgin Mary visiting the mountain home of her relative Elizabeth, an event that inspired the church's name. Wooden pews and nineteenth-century Stations of the Cross complete the effect, evoking the devotion of the faithful in the midst of the Big Bonanza. The stained-glass windows were originally an understated combination of clear glass with floral designs and limited, subdued color, but they were replaced in the latter half of the twentieth century with more vivid splashes of color. The church maintains a collection of Patrick Manogue's vestments embroidered with thread made of actual gold and silver, expressions of the wealth of the Comstock.

While it is well known that the center of town had to be rebuilt after the 1875 fire, understanding exactly what occurred can be more difficult. Clearly, hundreds of buildings were razed, but there were a surprising number of survivors within the boundaries of the disaster. A bird's-eye view, published shortly before the fire, is a useful tool when looking at Virginia City before October 26, 1875, and it provides evidence of what remained after the snowstorm. The building that now houses the Bucket of Blood Saloon on the southeast corner of Union and C Streets, for example, was at the heart of the catastrophe. The wooden parts of the structure were certainly destroyed, but its masonry, including a stout stone foundation—likely dating to the beginning of Virginia City— and its three stories of brick walls were sufficiently intact to allow their reuse.

Prominent victims of the fire included the pre-fire home of the *Territorial Enterprise,* a three-story masonry structure that dominated the uphill block of C Street and its neighbor, the International Hotel, which stood on the corner of Union and C Streets. The publisher of the *Gold*

Hill Daily News graciously offered to share his press with his rival so the *Enterprise* could continue to appear in print. But within weeks, the Comstock giant had relocated into the much smaller—but entirely adequate—brick building on the downhill side of C Street that still houses a remarkable print room and journalistic memorabilia from the nineteenth century. So much of this new site remained after the fire that only minimal reconstruction was needed to reestablish the *Enterprise*.

This structure became a point of confusion when the twentieth-century entrepreneurs Lucius Beebe and Charles Clegg purchased the property and the rights to the newspaper's name, restarting the revered institution as a weekly in 1952. Beebe and Clegg desperately wanted to capture the glory days of the *Enterprise*, and in particular the period when Mark Twain worked there. They consequently invented a history for their building, which suggested that it had been home to the newspaper as early as 1863. To add veracity to the claim, they printed a book in 1954, *The Comstock Commotion*, which described this fictional past. They then set aside an old wooden desk where Samuel Clemens supposedly wrote his articles and first assumed his pen name. It is an absurd tangle of history and myth, but there could be no better institution for this sort of fabrication than the *Enterprise*, home to so many tall tales during the heyday of Virginia City.

Aside from these few standing remnants, most of the heart of Virginia City was in ruins by the evening of October 26, 1875. One of the more devastating casualties was the multistoried courthouse that dominated the center of B Street. Not only was the civic heart of the community destroyed, but the flames also took much of the corporate memory of the mining industry. Countless records of land ownership and claims were gone. But even in this case there were some surprising survivors. Several safes had sheltered their contents from the fire, although many documents emerged with charred edges. Still, the loss was profound, and when the county sought to rebuild, there was a clear mandate for the new structure to include steel-lined, walk-in vaults to house records.

The choices behind the construction of a new courthouse reveal a great deal about the mind-set of the community after the fire. Insiders knew that while the Big Bonanza strike of 1873 had flooded the local economy with millions of dollars, no new ore bodies of any significance had been discovered. Given the tenuous nature of the mines, the Storey County commissioners might have exercised fiscal prudence when deciding to rebuild their courthouse. Instead they hired Kenitzer and Raun, a prominent San Francisco architectural firm, to draw up several designs for a new courthouse. Appearance was everything, and the commissioners were determined to paint the Comstock Mining District as thriving, with a booming economy. Ultimately, the town's leaders chose the plans that promised a monumental structure more magnificent than any other Nevada courthouse. The state's most expensive temple of justice—for the first fifty years of its history—was dedicated in early 1877. The public works project sent a clear signal that the Comstock community fathers believed the mines had a future and that the county was willing to back that belief with its own resources. The effect instilled confidence.

John Piper rebuilt his opera house, moving it from D Street to B Street and incorporating his 1863 brick business building, which survived the 1875 fire. The hall featured a horseshoe balcony and a flat floor, which could also serve as a dance floor and a roller rink. (Courtesy of the Bucket of Blood Saloon)

The conflagration of 1875 was not the first fire to destroy blocks of real estate in Virginia City, but it was the worst, and it is still referred to as the "Great Fire." When excavating in the center of town, whether for a building project, for the planting of a rosebush, or during the precise work of archaeologists, it is nearly impossible not to encounter a thick layer of black ash together with heaps of melted glass, charred wood, and twisted, rusted metal, all embraced by a greasy black grime that still exudes the scent of the fire. These remnants are provocative evidence of the disaster of October 26, 1875. The catastrophe survives, in some sense, hidden beneath the surface of the ground.

Within two years of the fire, Virginia City was rebuilt. The new International Hotel opened in 1877, soaring six stories above C Street and featuring luxurious appointments and the state's first commercial elevator. Piper moved his opera house, which also opened in 1877 but now located two blocks uphill, opposite the row of commercial establishments on the B Street side of the International. Throughout the central core of Virginia City, businesses thrived and new apartment buildings were occupied. In residential neighborhoods, new homes completed the impression that the mining district had recovered and was fully open for business. Although well outside the fire zone, the new Fourth Ward School joined many other establishments when it first opened its doors in 1877, providing much-needed classroom space in a town that had lost several schools to the devastation. Designed to house a thousand scholars, the majestic Second Empire structure at the south end of C Street was hailed as a monument to education. Its modern amenities included flush toilets and a ventilation and central heating system. The facility was billed as second to none on the Pacific Coast. Community leaders wanted, again, to send a message: the Comstock was thriving and the Fourth Ward School would stand as a testament to Virginia City's commitment to educating its young citizens in the finest style.

The restoration of Virginia City represented a financial boom for the building trades. Unfortunately, despite outward appearances, the enormous effort did not remedy the perennial problem that has plagued mining areas for millennia: viable ore is not a renewable resource, and when exploration fails to identify new deposits, a place like the Comstock is susceptible to an untimely end. From a historical perspective, it may be

The 1877 incarnation of the International Hotel was the grandest of all. Rising from the ashes of the fires of 1875, it was six stories on the C Street side and featured the first commercial elevator in Nevada, shops facing C and B Streets, and luxury rooms and apartments. (Courtesy of the Library of Congress, 93504914)

obvious that dark clouds were on the Comstock horizon, but that was not clear for those living through those years. For the next two decades the destiny of Virginia City was left to an unspoken debate between optimists and pessimists. Those who believed the Comstock would reveal viable ore stayed on; those who saw the slump as something more permanent left to pursue other opportunities.

Regardless of the mining district's future, life remained. Those who lingered contributed to the birth of legends that became the Comstock's legacy as much as the wealth of its bullion, and the reach of its folklore became as great as the effect of its vast discoveries. Richard James Jose provides an example of how the fabrications of the Comstock became entwined with an international star. Jose was born on June 5, 1862, in

Lanner, a village in the heart of Cornwall's mining district. His father worked underground, but when the elder Jose died in 1876, he left his widow and five children without an income. The widow sent her eldest son, Richard, to Virginia City to connect with an uncle who would presumably establish the young man in the American West. Unfortunately, Jose's uncle was nowhere to be found, and the Cornish immigrant had to fend for himself.

What followed is obscured by a jumble of inventions that has left history savaged in a way that rivals the fabrications crafted by the Comstock journalists—and yet the truth was no less impressive. Legend described Jose as a lad of some eight years, arriving with only a few coins in his pocket and with a tag pinned to his lapel so he could be properly delivered to his uncle. Jose was a singer, a countertenor, which meant his range was higher than most, and it may have been easy to pass himself off as much younger. He later insisted he was born in 1869 because a boy of eight made for a much more romantic story than the idea of someone near his fifteenth birthday—which was the case—arriving in a mining district noted for hiring workers that age.

Instead, Jose's modified biography transformed him into a hopeless, underage orphan left to sing for his fare in the rugged saloons of the Wild West town. Cornish miners recognized him as a vulnerable immigrant from their homeland, and when they heard his magical voice, they gave him enough money to support himself. But according to the legend, the town's respectable women could not abide an eight-year-old singing in saloons, so they forbade him from entering those establishments. He then fled to Carson City's taverns, with the same immediate success followed by the familiar reaction of morality-enforcing ladies. Jose subsequently settled in Reno, where he apprenticed with another uncle at an iron forge, but he still sang, and if the tale is to be believed, he became known as "the Singing Blacksmith."

Elements of this story are certainly accurate, but the reality of his actual age was less poignant than the one he later promoted. The singer's subsequent career is better documented, but there remained one last fabrication to be infused into Jose's biography. In the mid-1880s, he joined various traveling minstrel shows and earned a reputation as having a remarkable voice. Eventually, he became the leader of his own troupe of performers. But once again, the hold of the Comstock was such that no opportunity for falsehoods could be denied.

At some point, Jose changed his name to reflect a new ethnicity that the singer apparently believed would serve him better than his Cornish roots. Jose, pronounced like "rose," was a common enough Cornish name, but the performer changed it to José—"hoh-zay," with a Spanish flare—giving him a bogus Hispanic heritage. Sometimes his identity shift went so far that he was billed as Juan Ricardo José, and his biography told a story about his father coming from Spain and then leaving his child an orphan. Whether for marketing purposes or for some personal reason, Jose embraced this new account, adding yet another layer of fiction to an already extraordinary tale.

Not only did Jose have an outstanding career on the stage, but he also became a pathfinder in the entertainment industry. Although his high-pitched voice fell out of fashion as the twentieth century unfolded, his extensive range in the high registers was perfect for the time. Starting in 1903, Jose made a series of best-selling recordings that secured his place in the history of the music industry. His "Silver Threads among the Gold" became his signature piece and was the title song for a film that premiered at Madison Square Garden in 1915, the facility's first use as a motion picture theater. And as an additional innovation, Jose stood in the wings and sang the various tunes as his image flickered before the audience in this age of silent movies.

Although Jose's professional name and age were fabrications, his talent was very real, and he had a reasonable if not unassailable claim to being the world's first recording star. Like many who came to and left the Comstock, he embedded a bit of the mining district in his biography, in this case at its very foundation. Even today a fragment of this notable star lingers in Virginia City: Piper's Opera House displays a faded square of what was once a much larger, wall-sized poster publicizing a performance by the hometown star, Richard Jose.

Regardless of such anecdotes of success and unusual characters associated with Virginia City, the mining district was in decline. The decennial federal census provides a series of snapshots over time, evidence of a failing economy. In 1880, the population of Storey County, which included both Virginia City and Gold Hill, was 16,115. This was only a few years following the fire and after the production of the fabled Big Bonanza had peaked and then begun its decline. In the middle of the 1870s, the population of the county may have been as high as 25,000. Within a few years, the core of the district had shed up to 9,000 people, but that was only the beginning. In 1890, the population dwindled to 8,806, roughly 16,000 fewer people than at its peak. At the turn of the century, 3,673 people were living in the county. A few years later, a modest mining boom breathed life into the district: the population in 1910 was 3,045, but ten years later, the number of people calling Virginia City and Gold Hill home was halved. And by 1930, the census recorded only 667 residents in the county.

Facing the Comstock's decline, people in the mining district in 1880 could not imagine what would unfold in coming decades. The region had slumped before, and new discoveries had always reversed the hard

Famed western photographer Carleton Watkins visited Virginia City in 1876 and again in 1878, when he took this image. He captured a vibrant community that seemed poised to last forever. Buildings stand tightly packed in the center of town where fire had devastated the place only three years earlier. (Courtesy of the Comstock Historic District Commission)

times. It was well known that those who remained in the district were in the best position to profit from fresh periods of prosperity. The 1880 census provides vivid evidence of what it was like to live on the Comstock in the midst of decline. That year, enumerators recorded for the first time how many of the previous twelve months residents had spent unemployed. Young single men and those in the building trades suffered the most. More than that, there is evidence of how families without a stable income coped with the situation: the hillside above Virginia City was cluttered with abandoned shacks from the 1860s that now gave shelter to squatters waiting for better times. There was no running water and the hike up and down the hill to the main street was onerous. A closer look at the families who were camping out in this rustic circumstance reveals a poignant detail: most had only daughters or very young boys. Families with older boys were able to live in the center of town, presumably because the youngsters could scramble for odd jobs, while girls, restricted by proper Victorian society, had no means of bringing home additional income. Regardless of the circumstances, those living on the hillside eventually left during the 1880s as it became increasingly clear that the depression would be a long-lasting one.

Exploration continued through the early 1880s. Eventually, however, companies could no longer hemorrhage financially, and by the middle of the decade, pumping out the deeper shafts ceased. The Comstock came to rely on the passive draining at the 1,600-foot level provided by the Sutro Tunnel, meaning that the excavations below that point would be submerged. Optimists persisted, and miners continued to excavate on the Comstock through the turn of the century, but employment declined and profits were minimal or nonexistent.

Several benchmark events signaled how completely the chapter of the Comstock bonanza had closed. In 1897, the Daughters of Charity were allowed to leave their mission in Virginia City. For years, the numbers of children at their orphanage and patients in their hospital had declined. Support for their efforts was all but cut off, and the Daughters were left in what could only be described as destitution. When their order granted permission for them to move to another mission, the school closed and the hospital was handed over to the county for operation. It was a clear statement that the period of opulence had long since ended.

Correspondence preserved in the attic of a house speaks to another aspect of declining Comstock prospects. An Irish American man mining in Butte wrote to a cousin who remained in Virginia City, telling him that he should relocate because Comstockers were doing well in the Montana mining district, where copper was king. Wherever they went, most people who had enjoyed Virginia City's bonanza left as the economy continued to slump.

There is clear evidence that the Cornish immigrants were the first to leave the Comstock once mining seemed to have failed. Unlike their Irish counterparts, the Cornish rarely married while moving from one district to the next. Nearly three-quarters of the immigrants from Cornwall were miners, while only about 50 percent of the Irishmen worked underground on the Comstock. Cornish identity was tied to the occupation, whereas the Irish were apparently more willing to leave the industry and consider other sources of support.

The declining fortunes of the Comstock also signaled disaster for Gold Hill. Long the working-class home of a smaller population, Gold Hill had thriving mines during the heyday, but it was always in the shadow of the larger, more prosperous Virginia City. When the economy failed, the vast majority of Gold Hill residents either left or moved to Virginia City as the region contracted to a core of businesses and dwellings. The result of this process left fewer structures in Gold Hill, a town that had once boasted eight thousand people. Virginia City's business district and many of its homes endured the worst of the ensuing decades and survived to exploit better times when they finally arrived.

Chapter Five

The Irresistible Persistence of the Past

The story of Virginia City in the twentieth century is one of repeated reinterpretation of the place and its past. The century dawned, however, with the old tale retold—namely, with a mining boom. Perhaps appropriately, it was linked with a scam. A group of entrepreneurs and mine owners decided to pump out the water from the flooded north-end mines and launch an exploration for a new bonanza, with an eye toward capturing the support of investors while inspiring enthusiasm for the sale of stocks.

These organizers may have been as shocked as anyone when they actually discovered a viable ore body, launching a decade of mining productivity. The invention of cyanide ore processing contributed to the new success as it transformed once-marginal deposits into profitable resources. Even the old mill tailings were reworked with the new method. All of this combined with the 1903 central Nevada mining boom of Goldfield and Tonopah, which sent some of its gold-and-silver-laden rock for reduction at Comstock mills, enhancing the old district's reasserted prosperity.

In spite of this latter-day echo of an old story, most of the twentieth century would see the unfolding of unexpected possibilities. As the new mining boom faded during the second decade of the century, exploration continued. Developers cut or expanded local open pits. Others built cyanide mills, including one at the base of Six Mile Canyon and another, massive complex at American Flat, southwest of Virginia City. Ultimately, these efforts failed, but at the time it must have seemed that mining would be as much a part of the future of the district as it had been in the past.

Although a great deal of effort was made to advance mining, the industry failed to fuel another period of sustained prosperity. By the 1920s, the prospects of the Comstock faded once again. Being removed from the population centers of Reno and Carson City, Virginia City was threatened with extinction as it dwindled to little more than the last refuge of those who were too old to leave. Still, just as it became easy to imagine the district declining into a collection of ghost towns, fresh possibilities began to emerge.

The mining of nearby chalk deposits provided some with wages, but a good part of the local economy would come to rely on something other than the old model. Beginning in the 1930s, and increasing with every decade, bohemian artists, literati, and easterners became intrigued with Virginia City, seeing it as something of a refuge as well as an icon of the Wild West, which they could romanticize. In response to the tourist trade as it slowly emerged in the mid-twentieth century, locals opened businesses geared to meet this new demand. Early attempts at museums prefigured sophisticated later efforts. Saloons were more successful, however. Responding in part to Nevada's legalization of gambling in 1931, places such as the Delta Saloon and the Bucket of Blood Saloon laid the foundation that served these institutions well for the next eighty years— and beyond. At the same time, the New Deal Works Progress Administration reworked Geiger Grade, the road dating to the early 1860s that provided access to Virginia City from Reno. Tourism was modest by the standard established in future decades, but the influx of the curious was sufficient to provide an income for many residents.

In 1940, the Comstock Mining District enjoyed a renewed flash of fame, recalling the 1870s and the discovery of the Big Bonanza: the release of the motion picture *Virginia City* starring Errol Flynn, Miriam Hopkins, Humphrey Bogart, and Randolph Scott captured the nation's attention, if only for a moment. The mediocre film told an implausible story about a Confederate effort to steal Comstock bullion to support the rebellion of the South. Lucius Beebe, featured on the cover of *Life* in 1939 as the man who set the standard for the nation's fashion, joined other film critics and several stars to watch a premiere at Piper's Opera House in Virginia City.

Beebe hated the movie but found the place enchanting. In spite of being a child of the Boston Brahmins, the upper class that ruled the Massachusetts capital for decades, Beebe was a natural outcast. Wry and sarcastic, he boasted that he was the only person to have been expelled from both Yale and Harvard. And whether or not that was the case mattered little: Beebe had low regard for the facts. He cut a broad swath through eastern society and was surprisingly successful in spite of doing little to hide his homosexuality. Ultimately, the flamboyant Beebe was drawn to the West and its perceived freedom.

When Beebe's younger partner, Charles Clegg, received an honorable discharge from the U.S. Navy after World War II, the two men moved

A book-signing party in 1949 in Virginia City's Delta Saloon attracted several notable authors of the West. Shown here in the foreground from left to right are Duncan Emrich (folklorist), Walter Van Tilburg Clark (writer, kneeling), Roger Butterfield (historian, standing), Irene Bruce (poet, seated), Charles Glegg (writer), Marian Emrich (folklorist), and Lucius Beebe (writer). (Courtesy of the Bucket of Blood Saloon)

to Virginia City. Entranced by nineteenth-century railroads, the couple rode in their own Pullman car, which they decorated in full Victoriana and named the "Gold Coast." The transcontinental rails took them across the United States, an event that some suggest inspired the 1960s television show *Wild Wild West*. Again, it does not matter whether or not this is true: Beebe epitomized the standard of the Comstock, embracing the notion that a well-told falsehood was better than a boring fact. The two gentlemen wore costumes and otherwise appeared in every way to anticipate the theatrical Artemus Gordon and the athletic James T. West of the popular TV series. At Reno, the railroad transferred their Gold Coast to the Virginia and Truckee, the fabled short line, and it was a V&T engine that hauled Beebe and Clegg to Carson City. Unfortunately, the rails were scavenged during the war, so the couple could not arrive in Virginia City in the style they had imagined, but arrive they did, and the Comstock was never the same.

Beebe and Clegg revitalized Virginia City as though it were their own private mining boom. They purchased and restored property around town. Most importantly, as mentioned earlier, they acquired the *Territorial Enterprise* building, which they opened as a museum and as the focus of what would become an important weekly newspaper. The pair published a series of books celebrating the Comstock's past and combined these with articles in the *Territorial Enterprise* written by diverse literary figures of the West. Their efforts shined a new spotlight on the mining district.

People throughout the region began to take note. Although this was not the famed nineteenth-century era of Bonanza mining, something important nevertheless stirred in Virginia City. The Comstock's bright flame once again attracted a wide variety of people, but there was a difference. Writers A. J. Liebling and Roger Butterfield, along with the poet Irene Bruce, came to call Virginia City home at one time or another. The Katies—Katie Hillyer and her partner, Katie Best—also settled there. The couple occupied what was known as the Spite House on D Street, so called because the twentieth-century interpreters falsely imagined that a house built too close to its neighbor, cutting off light to the first home's windows, must have been located there out of malice. The Katies added their own brand of color to the Comstock scene. Hillyer, reporting on a

Katie Hillyer and her partner, Katie Best, lived in a D Street home known as the Spite House. During the 1860s and 1870s, Virginia City homes were frequently constructed wall to wall. During the early twentieth century, it was common for the remaining residents to purchase a neighbor's property for back taxes and to subsequently cannibalize the structure for firewood, leaving an open yard on the side. The few houses that remained with the original close configuration became curiosities, and people explained them with local folklore that suggested the property owner had built his home so close to spite his neighbor. (Photograph by Ronald M. James)

demonstration of a new military vehicle for the *Washington Daily News* in early 1941, is credited as the first journalist to record the term "Jeep." The Katies went on to brave wartime London to report on the Blitz, after which they settled in Virginia City to enjoy a quieter life, but one still filled with writing.

Duncan Emrich was another among the assortment of characters drawn to Virginia City. Born in 1908 to missionaries in Turkey, Emrich earned a Ph.D. from Harvard under the medievalist George Lyman Kittredge, an intellectual legacy that ensured that Emrich would also understand folklore. During World War II, Emrich became an intelligence officer on General Eisenhower's staff. With peacetime, he was named the director of the Archive of American Folk Song in the Library of Congress. Emrich then established that institution's Folklore Section, administering the program until 1955, after which he joined the Foreign

Service as a cultural affairs officer, serving at a number of embassies. In 1969 he became an adjunct professor of folklore at American University. Throughout these travels, Emrich was consistently drawn to Virginia City, which he visited as early as the 1930s. He frequently summered on the Comstock, using some of his time to collect oral tradition. Emrich's poorly recorded interviews of locals conducted in the Delta Saloon in 1949 and 1950 provide some extraordinarily valuable recollections of people who would have otherwise been silenced by the grave. Between collecting, drinking (he liked Old Crow, 100 proof), and getting married at least once (the Silver Dollar Saloon was his favorite for drinking and weddings), Emrich joined the pantheon of national luminaries that became the hallmark of postwar Virginia City. The town grew into a peculiar phenomenon, part bohemian enclave and part tourist attraction as people took to the road during summer vacations. With Emrich's death in 1977, the Comstock lost one of its remarkable citizens.

More locally based but also nationally famous, Walter Van Tilburg Clark came to Nevada as a child with his father, who became president of the University of Nevada in Reno. The younger Clark moved away to teach English at a variety of posts, but mostly he worked on his fiction writing. Clark gained fame for *The Ox-Bow Incident*, which appeared in 1940. This tale ranks among the first novels in the genre known as the modern Western, maturing beyond the clichés and formulas that had dominated the fiction of the Wild West since the time of the dime novel. *The Ox-Bow Incident* and *The Track of the Cat* (1949) became films of some renown. In 1962, Clark returned to Nevada permanently, although his roots had always remained in the state and especially on the Comstock. He took a writer-in-residence position at the University of Nevada at Reno, but Virginia City became the focus of the last nine years of his life. Clark died in 1971 before completing his final project, assembling the diaries of prominent Comstock journalist Alfred Doten, the nineteenth-century editor of the *Gold Hill Daily News*.

A critical turning point in the history of Virginia City tourism occurred in the late 1940s, but to properly understand the dynamics of how things changed, it is necessary to return to the beginning of the decade and examine the effects of the war. Shortly after the bombing of Pearl Harbor, President Roosevelt issued an executive order prohibiting the use of strategic resources for the mining of precious metals. While it did not require an end to gold and silver mining, the order strangled the industry by cutting off its supply of fuel and other necessary materials. Virginia City consequently lost one of the major avenues for its return to economic viability.

At the same time, the Western Defense Command under the authority of the U.S. Army ordered western governors to close brothels within a fifty-mile radius of military bases in response to federal legislation. Reno quickly complied with the directive. In areas farther removed from the major routes of transportation, especially those not seeking or expecting War Department investment in defense-related facilities, there was no requirement to place a handful of local women out of work, particularly when they might attract outsiders to bars and gambling tables.

In Virginia City, the few prostitutes still there remained in business, though they may have attempted to be a little more discreet. North of the Truckee Meadows, the Reno Army Air Base, eventually known as Stead Air Force Base, was established in 1942. Almost immediately, the personnel from the base formed convoys to visit Virginia City, ostensibly because of an interest in mining history and to attend lemonade socials and band concerts. Testimony from those recalling the period paints a different picture, suggesting that the young men were more interested in drinking and gambling on C Street. And then there were the brothels on D Street. Saloons obligingly kept civilian clothes on hand so servicemen could change and visit the prostitutes without being identified as part of the war effort. When word of this reached authorities in San Francisco, they put pressure on Storey County, which passed an anti-prostitution ordinance in the spring of 1944. It is unclear whether the new rule was enforced. Brothels, after all, were still there a year later when the war ended, and the prostitutes represented an essential component of Virginia City's economy.

Following victory in 1945, the Reno Army Air Base closed temporarily. With war's end, gas and tire rationing also ended, resulting in a slow but steady increase of tourists coming to see the old icon of the Wild West. Prostitution, which had attracted visitors to Virginia City in the first decades of the twentieth century, now became a liability. A crisis occurred in July 1947 when Tony Harvey and Louis Barton—both local brothel owners—fought over Harvey's new wife, Kay O'Brien, who had been a prostitute and madam. Gunfire ensued, wounding both men, at which point Harvey returned to his house on D Street and hanged himself. Authorities investigating the scene also found a shallow grave containing the body of Rose, Harvey's previous wife and a former prostitute.

The sordid story was great for headlines but not for tourism, and it sparked a debate in the community. At one point, opponents pointed out that Nevada state law prohibited brothels from operating within a certain distance of schools. They argued that the D Street prostitutes had been in violation of the requirement since the 1937 opening of a school in the center of Virginia City. To this, Lucius Beebe famously quipped, "Move the school, keep the girls!" The enthusiast of the Wild West would naturally take the side of a nineteenth-century institution he felt added flavor to the community, but times had changed and the new economy demanded action. In August 1947, Storey County once again passed an ordinance banning prostitution. It was not entirely effective: older residents indicate that the house on the southwest corner of D and Sutton Streets remained in business until the end of the decade, but the establishment was far enough away from the tourists—and the school—that it was perhaps easier to overlook.

Regardless of how bumpy the road was, the path for Virginia City led directly to tourism, and with each year more people arrived to sample a bit of the authentic Old West. Institutions like the Bucket of Blood Saloon and the Delta Saloon with its modest casino combined with homegrown private museums and antiques stores to provide the commodities that this new source of income sought. Visitors arrived in increasing numbers throughout the 1950s, and it was easy to imagine a promising future for the historic mining capital.

Ironically, just as the Comstock ended its long history of prostitution, it began to further exploit the subject. Julia Bulette, murdered and then placed on a pedestal in local folklore, became commercialized as an ideal of frontier femininity. Bulette's story was now publicized as a means to titillate tourists while the community preserved a sense of decorum by prohibiting the business that supported her.

At the same time, Don McBride, of the Bucket of Blood, joined forces with a few others to construct a gravesite for Julia Bulette in the Flowery Cemetery. Her actual final resting place was unknown by the mid-twentieth century, but Virginia City needed a place to celebrate an emerging legend. The white picket fence of her new—and empty—gravesite was visible with the aid of a coin-operated telescope at the back of the Bucket of Blood Saloon, enhancing the fabrication that Bulette was buried there because she was shunned by those who wished to reserve the Silver Terrace Cemeteries for respectable people. In fact, the Silver Terrace Cemeteries, the better-known final resting place of Virginia City's residents, was not ready for burials until after Bulette's murder. It made for a good story, but it was a tale that needed an actual location, so constructing Bulette's gravesite where none existed added to her marketability.

This first period of postwar tourism reached its peak as Beebe, Clegg, and the rest of the community anticipated the 1959 centennial of the

Julia Bulette's imagined grave site dated to the mid-twentieth century. Locals promoted the site to tourists as the final resting place of the "best prostitute of the West." It remains a fixture in local folklore: people often decorate the tree behind the white picket fence with dolls and other items. (Photograph by Ronald M. James)

discovery of the Comstock Lode. The U.S. Postal Service issued a commemorative stamp depicting the discovery of ore on June 8, 1859, and this was at a time when such honors were much more rare than a few decades later. Vice President Richard Nixon, his Nevada-born wife, Pat, and their two daughters attended a dedication ceremony for a monument that still stands in the parking lot of the Delta Saloon in the center of town.

As part of the fun in 1959, the *Territorial Enterprise* reported on the first annual camel race in Virginia City. Beebe and Clegg must have been satisfied that their weekly publication had gained prominence and influence when other newspapers gave accounts of the contest. And the editors must have been particularly pleased because there had been no camel race. By hoodwinking the region, they revived the old tradition of the journalistic hoax. It seemed that the Old West was alive and well.

Yet something totally unpredictable loomed on the horizon. Throughout the 1950s, the Comstock pieced together meager means of support while slowly building on a modest tourism trade. The period is not unlike one hundred years earlier, when placer miners worked Gold Canyon while a fortune waited to be discovered. Echoing the great strikes of 1859, in September 1959 the National Broadcasting Company premiered *Bonanza*. Black-and-white Westerns were a popular staple of 1950s television, and NBC had been looking for a vehicle to promote sales of color TVs produced by its parent company, RCA. The centennial celebration of the Comstock attracted the attention of the network's producers, who hoped to capture viewers with the reliable genre of the Western, now presented in vivid color. The show's writers drew inspiration for story lines from Virginia City's lively history. While Beebe and Clegg could take pride in how they had helped to turn the Comstock into a household name, they were appalled by the consequences. The following summer, tourists began arriving in numbers far exceeding those of previous years. They filled the streets and businesses with an intrusion that some residents believed ruined the rustic, remote feel of the Old West, which had been so well preserved by the seclusion of the Comstock.

More importantly, this new wave of tourists put pressure, largely unspoken, on local property owners to transform the appearance of their buildings so that their structures would look more like the Virginia City that Ben, Adam, Hoss, and Little Joe Cartwright would recognize, and less like the authentic brick-and-iron buildings of the industrial capital that it actually was. Facades made of vertical pecky cedar began appearing along the main commercial corridor, hiding vintage structures. New construction favoring the Wild West, *Bonanza* style continued the destruction of the authentic dignified period architecture, which had suffered from years of neglect and deterioration. And all of this was happening just as the National Park System recognized the old mining district in 1961 with National Historic Landmark status.

One of the first serious efforts to preserve the remarkable resources of Virginia City dates to the 1940s, long before the crisis that followed in the wake of the television show. To halt the trend leading toward the degradation of the historic district, community leaders from Reno organized to preserve the town's icons, including the Fourth Ward School. This group also advocated the creation of an architectural review committee to be imposed on local property owners. As early as April 5, 1949, the *Nevada Appeal* was able to report the adoption of a Storey County ordinance and the formation of a nine-member planning commission that would regulate construction in Virginia City. The article declared that the "annual tourist flood makes even Boothill cemetery a busy crossroads" and that the plans for restoration would be directed by the "Virginia City Foundation Trust." Locals disliked having their community burial ground—which still serves as the local cemetery—called "Boothill," but most welcomed any attempt to preserve the town. According to the article, there would not be a single master fund, but rather "individual building sponsorship." Unfortunately, the sponsors who would help with the repair of other buildings failed to materialize.

A renewed attempt, inspired by the Nevada statehood centennial in 1964, resulted in a restoration committee that had ambitions to take on many projects. Ultimately, the endeavor began and ended, once again, with the Fourth Ward School, saving at least that one monument. Although the community failed to find a use for the school, the preservation effort allowed the icon to remain standing for two more decades as it waited for yet another round of restoration. The celebration of Virginia City's heritage in the 1960s culminated with a state law, passed in 1969 and amended several times, that established what would become the Comstock Historic District Commission, a citizens' committee that reviews building activity within the district. In February 1971, a precursor of the commission was able to submit its third report indicating that work was nearly complete on the restoration of the Fourth Ward School, an effort that had generated "more than $60,000 worth of labor and materials . . . contributed to this project by building contractors, suppliers and labor unions from the Reno area." The donations meant that more than a third of the original 1965 legislative appropriation of $15,000 for the restoration of the school was left unexpended and available for additional work, but surviving records do not reveal what happened to the remaining funds.

The trend of the 1960s to rusticate the Comstock, transforming it into a Wild West caricature, drew to a close, and over subsequent decades, television-inspired architecture slowly gave way to more appropriate design and restoration. By the second decade of the twenty-first century, the only survivor of the "Cartwright" era in Virginia City was the Bonanza Casino on C Street. With its cedar facade, the structure is a significant and rare example that recalls an important postwar period of Comstock history.

While offering visitors inexpensive, faux western buildings, businessmen applied the same strategy to the products they sold: Virginia City became known for its hot dogs—forever turning on heated metal rollers—and T-shirts. Just as the previous century's mining was balanced on margins, the tourism industry of the 1960s and 1970s marketed the cheapest possible products to as many people as possible for the maximum return. Bad winters inhibited travel to Virginia City, and decades of baby boomers restricted family vacations to the summer months when children were out of school. This increased the cost of operation as the community sat largely dormant for much of the year, waiting for the return of warmth and the carloads of tourists.

In the previous century, ore bodies were viable only if the cost of the excavation, milling, and infrastructure did not exceed the value of the bullion produced. Similarly, modern entrepreneurs minimized the cost of the product—whether food, cheap clothing with tacky images, or breakable plastic toys—so that tourists could be processed and stripped of their bullion. Satisfaction did not matter. The television show

Bonanza lasted for years, and the waves of seasonal tourists it inspired seemed endless. These modern Comstock miners treated tourists like ore—nonrenewable resources that did not need to be cultivated because each season brought even more visitors.

Part of Virginia City's magic is its ability to reinvent itself. Television and the promotion of the Wild West provided a new chapter in a sequence of twentieth-century phases that included the art and literary crowd, the early attempts at museum development, and then ultimately the welcoming of the hundreds of thousands who repeatedly asked about the location of the Ponderosa, the ranch house of television's fictional Cartwrights.

Yet another Comstock digression took the form of an experiment with rock and roll. An unexpected turn of events occurred in 1965. The Charletons, a newly formed San Francisco band, decided to spend the summer in Virginia City, performing at the Red Dog Saloon on the north end of C Street. The group had not clearly defined itself, but instinct led it to dress in Victoriana or Wild West attire. And the members clearly agreed that the psychedelic drug LSD was central to the band's sound. Their presence added to an odd mix of old-time Comstockers, Cartwright-inspired tourists, and young people who were experimenting with Bay Area hippie personas. By chance—and as it often happens on the Comstock—the Virginia City sojourn of the Charletons helped spawn some key elements of the nation's music scene. During that summer of 1965, band members Mike Ferguson and George Hunter produced what is regarded as the first psychedelic poster advertising a rock concert. Called "The Seed," this work of art became the inspiration for a decade's worth of defining images associated with rock and youth culture. Because the musicians experimented with LSD while performing, the Charletons are often called the first acid-rock band, although their sound was far removed from what that genre later became. In addition, the Charletons introduced the first light show associated with a concert, and their venue sponsored the earliest dancing in conjunction with live rock music. These features combined to become one of the most important steps toward forming what would be known as the San Francisco Sound, all of it happening two hundred miles to the east in Virginia City.

With the end of the television show *Bonanza* in 1973, interest in

Virginia City began to wane. The winding down of each summer now inspired a seasonal cycle of complaint about diminished profits as business owners grew increasingly nostalgic for the glory days when the Cartwrights rode into America's living rooms every Sunday night. Yet the core of the old mining district survived in spite of the loss caused by time and neglect along with the turmoil and change that *Bonanza* inspired.

At the same time, some institutions were actually reborn. Beebe and Clegg were able to revive the *Territorial Enterprise,* complete with its national reputation and its penchant for hoaxes, but that was not all. In the 1980s, Louise Driggs, a descendant of John Piper, began a concert series in the old Opera House, featuring some of the finest performances anyone could hope to find in the nation, including the premiere of a late violin composition by Efrem Zimbalist Sr. Gradual restoration of private property occurred throughout the latter half of the twentieth century, encouraged by federal tax credits administered by the State Historic Preservation Office and the National Park Service. The infusion of state bond funds from the Nevada Commission for Cultural Affairs resulted in millions of dollars of restoration on the Comstock, inspiring other property owners to improve the condition of their historic buildings.

In the midst of all this change, the old story of prostitution and its association with Virginia City had yet another unfolding chapter. The profession had produced the legend of Julia Bulette, the prostitute murdered in 1867 and subsequently celebrated for twentieth-century tourists. But there were many others whose stories had once resonated on the Comstock: Jessie Lester, the madam who died following a Christmastime attack in 1864, and the more successful nineteenth-century lives of Cad Thompson and Jenny Tyler, who ran prominent houses throughout the first period of Comstock prosperity. Then there was the tale of the Harvey suicide in 1947.

By the 1970s, prostitution was about to yield its most famous episode. After previous failed attempts at operating a brothel along the Truckee River in places that may or may not have been outside Storey County, Joe Conforte, an Italian immigrant born in 1926, served two terms in prison. Finally, in 1967, he took over the management of the Mustang Bridge Ranch, a brothel later known simply as the Mustang Ranch. This new phase of local prostitution was well removed from Virginia City geographically, but it was still in Storey County, and its political influence was profound. In 1971, Storey County legalized prostitution, taking advantage of a Nevada law that gave rural governments that option. This opened up a period of nearly two decades during which Conforte virtually controlled the county.

The Mustang Ranch became the center of scandal with a murder at the brothel, accusations of tax evasion, and various other charges and allegations. Ultimately, there was a plea bargain that failed to live up to the expectations of the prosecutor, inspiring Conforte to flee to Brazil in 1991. At the time of this writing, he was still living there, a senior citizen and a notorious fugitive from the nation's judicial system. Before he left, however, the brothel owner donated a significant amount of money, in quarterly installments, to the restoration of the Fourth Ward School, presumably in an effort to demonstrate that he was as community-minded as any businessman. For the most part, none of these events played a direct role in the Virginia City story, but the influence of what happened in the "River District" was felt throughout the region, especially when it came to the politics of Storey County government.

Prostitution, however, was merely a distraction. First and last, the Comstock is a mining district. As if the soul of the old Comstock refused to be laid to rest, the industry has been part of the community for practically every decade since 1849. It came back to life in the late 1970s with the excavation of the Houston Mineral and Oil open pit in Gold Hill. The end result surpassed the scale of what had occurred previously on the surface of the Comstock. Open pits in the district date to 1859, and there were significant efforts to develop them during the 1920s and 1930s, but nothing equaled the size of this new phase of mining. Houston Mineral and Oil abandoned the district in 1982 after leaving a hole hundreds of feet deep and wide with slumping sidewalls and without a hint of reclamation. The Texas-based company became a symbol of what modern mining represented at its worst. When a smaller operation threatened to open near Silver City in the mid-1980s, local residents led a charge to stop the enterprise, but the falling value of gold had more to do with the retreat of the venture than any local resistance.

While the old industry occasionally came back to life, the earliest

Houston Mineral and Oil stopped excavation of its enormous Gold Hill pit in 1982, but the scar remains. (Courtesy of the Comstock Historic District Commission)

phase of mining left yet another legacy to ponder. Tests by the Environmental Protection Agency found traces of mercury downstream from some mill sites. Within the confines of the original mining district, those remnants of the past were surprisingly scarce. The Carson River was not so fortunate, but agency officials concluded that for the most part, retrieval of old mercury from deep within the riverbed would fail to eliminate all the contamination and would stir up the poisonous metal, to the detriment of the wildlife that now thrives on the drainage system.

A different manifestation of the mining industry's legacy also appears on occasion: on October 1, 1992, a forty-foot-wide sinkhole opened up in front of Virginia City's Hugh Gallagher Elementary School, taking with it the principal's 1988 Mercury Cougar; on August 11, 1995, the Osbiston Shaft, near the high school, opened and eventually consumed the beautifully crafted granite foundation for the hoist work. Events like these inspire questions as to whether the Comstock communities might someday sink into the ground, but sinkholes are, in fact, rare in hard-rock mining districts. Eastern coal mining removes large seams of coal only a few hundred feet from the surface. Subsequent rain erodes unstable swaths of land, and widespread collapse can occur. On the Comstock, most mining took place with a limited number of shafts reaching straight down hundreds of feet to excavations that were less extensive than those found in coal mining, and workers tended to drill into harder rock than their eastern counterparts. In addition, nineteenth-century miners frequently used waste material to fill abandoned underground chambers, adding stability to the hillside. Shafts may open in the future, but these events are typically confined to a small area.

In addition to everything else that unfolded as the twentieth century ended and a new millennium began, even the Virginia and Truckee Railroad enjoyed a new chapter, in spite of the tremendous obstacles its latter-day owners faced. Metal scrapers, desperate to feed the needs of the defense industry during World War II, had pulled up the track at the Virginia City end of the line, which had been abandoned by that time. Someone even removed the heavy timber supports for at least one of the tunnels. To resuscitate the railroad, the owners would need to lay new rails, engineer the crossing of a state highway, and purchase and maintain equipment. It was no easy task, but in the late 1970s, service was renewed between Virginia City and Gold Hill.

In the midst of all these advances, a few local enthusiasts set their sights on yet another local railroad resource. With the termination of the Virginia and Truckee Railroad services on May 31, 1950, the company's youngest engine began a strange final journey. The large black early-twentieth-century steam-driven beast was known only as #27, the romantic days of naming locomotives having passed. It appeared in a minor film and then the engine's owners donated it to the Nevada governor. Number 27 was subsequently put on display at two Carson City locations until 1971, when it was moved to Virginia City for outdoor exhibition at Union and E Streets, the location of the original rail yards. By the 1990s, the relic had languished, exposed to the elements for decades. Since track had been re-laid from Virginia City to Gold Hill and the V&T was back in service, some citizens felt the time was right to refit #27 so it could run once again.

Work began in a preliminary way, attracting the attention of the Nevada State Railroad Museum, which maintained that it, in fact, owned the locomotive. Against local protest, lawyers argued the case, to the satisfaction of state officials, that the original donation of the engine was to the governor, and the state did consequently have ownership. The museum asserted that it would take the engine to Carson City for restoration and a protected indoor display. A few residents decided that possession was a powerful argument. They transported #27 to Gold Hill, arranging it in a way that they believed would make removal most difficult. Rumors began to circulate that the relic had been booby-trapped with explosives and that sharpshooters were taking to the hills to hinder any attempt to take the engine.

When museum officials arrived for the move of the locomotive, they were escorted by Nevada Highway Patrol officers with rifles in case a firefight ensued. Workers searched carefully for explosives, and locals collectively shook their heads in disbelief that the threats had been taken seriously. The expert railroad museum staff proceeded with the restoration in Carson City while Comstockers protested that they had been deprived of a valuable means to interpret the past to tourists. Governor Bob Miller consequently promised that #27 would return to Virginia City, provided that an appropriate shelter could be built.

Resentment over the abduction of #27 festered until 2005, when the Comstock Historic District Commission opened a new facility on E Street, near the original location of Engine #27's display. John Copoulos, a Carson City architect, drew inspiration from a V&T car shed that had once stood only a few feet to the north of the building. His design featured a hall that was long enough to accommodate #27. As the facility neared completion, the Nevada State Railroad Museum staff suggested an exchange: they would display #27 since they did not have a good example of that type of engine, and Virginia City would be able to exhibit #18, the Dayton. Built in 1873, the Dayton was a glamorous, beautifully fitted, classic nineteenth-century locomotive from the days of the Big Bonanza. It had actually served Virginia City and was, in addition, the star of several early Hollywood movies. In contrast, #27 had never ventured up to Virginia City because it was too long and would have torn up track when making some of the tighter turns in the right-of-way. Besides all of that, #18 was a rare survivor of the Sacramento Central Pacific shops, giving it national significance. The Comstock clearly had the better end of the bargain although a few private protests were voiced. Some falsely believed that had #27 returned, they could have gained access to the state-owned building and realized the dream of returning it to operation.

But the Virginia and Truckee story did not end there. The Nevada Commission for the Reconstruction of the V&T Railway was able to lay track to Mound House in 2009, creating a terminus near Carson City's Highway 50. The Gold Hill Depot—one of the last standing structures associated with the V&T—was lovingly restored, providing yet another expression of the rejuvenation. The Virginia & Truckee Railroad Company continues to take passengers on a ride into Nevada's past, when the Comstock Lode and its famous railroad captured the imagination of the world. The route, now opened from Mound House to Virginia City, provides a view of the mining district unavailable to most visitors for over six decades.

Slowly, the old destructive ways of the tourism boom faded and a new approach emerged. By the late twentieth and early twenty-first centuries, there was a growing awareness that tourists could become a renewable resource if treated with respect and given a quality experience. Many in the community developed approaches that offered visitors a view of the past that was both accurate and exciting while reaching for a national standard of professionalism. The Fourth Ward School at the south end of C Street reopened in 1986, transforming eventually into a nationally acclaimed museum that includes a research archive. Also on C Street, the Nevada Gambling Museum offers a first-rate experience, and upgrades were made to the Comstock Firemen's Museum. In addition, parishioners opened a museum at St. Mary in the Mountains Catholic Church on E Street. A local historical marker program, along with the efforts of the Comstock Cemetery Foundation's restoration at the various Comstock burial grounds, has combined with professional programming and interpretation, and a steadily improving script for the local trolley tour to provide a better overall experience for the visitor.

At the same time, Virginia City residents explored approaches including the idea that a fabricated history was more important than authentically presenting and interpreting remnants of the past. Cowboy gunslingers—rare in the nineteenth century—began roaming the streets, always ready to take offense, shooting one another, and dying repeatedly, all in the name of entertainment. Opponents of this staged presentation of a romanticized Wild West were often heard to remark that the use of live ammunition rather than blanks would increase authenticity and excitement while discouraging the playacting. Others promoted the idea that ghosts haunted the Comstock's old buildings, sometimes inspiring cable television coverage of their exploits. In addition, seasonal gatherings of thousands of motorcyclists descending on Virginia City caused the community's focus for its events to shift to beer and black leather, chasing away family-based tourists for at least a few weekends. These experiments have had varying success and are not to be diminished, but national studies have been clear that honest, accurate depictions of the past attract more people and garner more financial rewards than inaccurate gimmickry. And shops featuring quality jewelry, fairly valued collectible antiques, or fossils and polished rare stones have tended to last longer than those selling rubber western knives and cheap felt hats, the kind of products that appealed to visitors in the 1960s.

In 1993, Billy Varga, who called himself—with some justification—the last of the underground miners, played a part in an event that demonstrated that much of the old Comstock was still alive and well. One night in August his house exploded, shattering windows in surrounding homes and sending a mining drill several blocks uphill to crush a vintage Cadillac. Varga maintained that a malfunctioning microwave set off some of his private collection of dynamite. Whether or not his explanation was true, the incident revealed to all concerned that Varga had stored explosives inappropriately in a place of residence, endangering himself and his neighbors. The incident recalled how Jacob Van Bokkelin and several others died, a hundred and twenty years before when a cache of dynamite exploded.

Of perhaps more interest was the community reaction to the incident. The next morning, a helicopter flying for the Nevada Division of Forestry was out to look at unrelated fire damage when the passengers asked if they could pass over Virginia City to look at the results of the Varga explosion. Within a few hours, local folklore maintained that the white and green helicopter was in fact black and belonged to the Bureau of Alcohol, Tobacco, and Firearms. Many people in Virginia City suspected that federal law enforcement was about to descend on the town to seize its private holdings of arms and explosives. By noon on the day following the explosion, several businesses along C Street sported "Don't Tread on Me" flags as signs of solidarity against a federal invasion that was never considered and would never happen.

The price of gold climbed in the early twenty-first century, inspiring mining to resume a role in the local landscape, once again linking the modern Comstock with its past. In 2010, Comstock Mining, Inc., began drilling exploration to identify new ore bodies for open-pit mining within the Virginia City National Historic Landmark District. Proposed activity was below Gold Hill, so the only community directly affected was Silver City. Not surprisingly, many nearby residents objected. Comstock Mining promised to set aside funds for reclamation and for the preservation of historic resources. Projects planned or undertaken by the time this book went to press include a grant to the Comstock Cemetery Foundation and the Historic Fourth Ward School Museum, along with the restoration of the Yellow Jacket hoisting works in Gold Hill. The company also conducted emergency stabilization of at least one of the local mills. Although Comstock Mining became the single largest employer within the historic district, it remains to be seen whether future excavation will have a positive or negative effect on Virginia City and the rest of the historic resource. It is probably fair to say that most area residents welcomed the enterprise, the economic boom it represented, and the rejuvenation of local mining. Since the industry will not simply abandon viable ore, what remains to be addressed is the nature of the undertaking and its relationship to the historic resource, the residents who live in the district, and those who visit this outstanding place.

Walking Tour

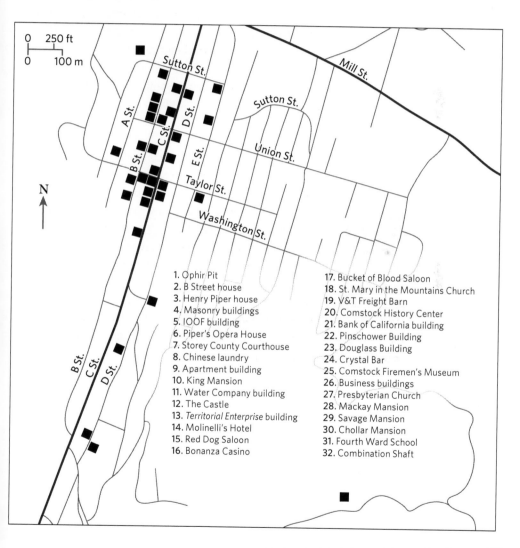

0 — 250 ft
0 — 100 m

N

Sutton St.
Sutton St.
Mill St.
Union St.
Taylor St.
Washington St.

A St.
B St.
C St.
D St.
E St.

B St.
C St.
D St.

1. Ophir Pit
2. B Street house
3. Henry Piper house
4. Masonry buildings
5. IOOF building
6. Piper's Opera House
7. Storey County Courthouse
8. Chinese laundry
9. Apartment building
10. King Mansion
11. Water Company building
12. The Castle
13. *Territorial Enterprise* building
14. Molinelli's Hotel
15. Red Dog Saloon
16. Bonanza Casino

17. Bucket of Blood Saloon
18. St. Mary in the Mountains Church
19. V&T Freight Barn
20. Comstock History Center
21. Bank of California building
22. Pinschower Building
23. Douglass Building
24. Crystal Bar
25. Comstock Firemen's Museum
26. Business buildings
27. Presbyterian Church
28. Mackay Mansion
29. Savage Mansion
30. Chollar Mansion
31. Fourth Ward School
32. Combination Shaft

The significance of the Comstock story aside, Virginia City and the other communities of the mining district are also remarkable because they are =living places with hundreds of historic buildings surviving from the glory days of the 1860s and 1870s. Every community has a past, and at least some remnants of what went before often survive. The Comstock is an extraordinary place, however, where most of what can be seen dates to that first twenty-year period when the district was important to the nation, if not the world.

In recognition of its pivotal history and the degree of its preservation, the secretary of the interior designated Virginia City and its neighbors as a National Historic Landmark district in 1961. The term "landmark" is often misunderstood and misused. Town and county commissions in every state designate local landmarks, and so the term has often come to mean something more humble than what is implied by federal law and national practice. The National Park Service maintains the National Register of Historic Places and above that, there is a list of National Historic Landmarks. More than eighty thousand sites are listed in the National Register, most of which have state or local significance. To qualify as a National Historic Landmark, a place must have national importance as well as outstanding integrity. Fewer than three thousand sites have received this recognition, and the Comstock, at fourteen thousand acres, is one of the largest (many locals incorrectly claim it is the largest).

The National Park Service has afforded Virginia City some sort of historic designation since the 1930s, because this capital of mining was critical to the nation in the nineteenth century and because so much of the past still endures, unblemished by the following decades. That having been said, a great deal that once stood in Virginia City is nevertheless gone. Nothing more than a trace survives of more than half of the buildings, and too many structures have been altered, but nowhere in the world is this not the case to some degree. No place preserves everything: fire and neglect take their toll, and rebuilding and remodeling are natural consequences of life itself. With these caveats in mind, a walk through Virginia City is like stepping into a time machine.

1 A good place to begin a tour is on the corner of B and Sutton Streets, in the northwest section of town. Ambitious walkers will hike the three blocks uphill on Sutton to an open area where early diggings are overgrown by locust trees and piñon pines. This is the Ophir Pit, the site of the original strike in June 1859. By drawing imaginary lines to connect the edges of the historic open-pit mine, it is possible to visualize how the original hillside might have looked

1 ■ Ophir Pit

2 ■ B Street house

3 ■ Henry Piper house

in the 1850s. On June 8, 1859, somewhere in what is now midair, McLaughlin and O'Riley first discovered the northern outcropping of the Comstock Lode as it breached the surface with an incredible amount of gold and silver. Within a few weeks, miners had excavated the beginnings of the pit, but what survives today is the result of generations of reworking the site. Miners have repeatedly enlarged the excavation looking for easy-to-reach gold and silver deposits. By 1860, it was clear that the sidewalls would collapse if workers dug deeper, and that is why underground mining began. Today, it is still possible to recognize the dynamics that inspired the transition.

2 Many historic homes survive to the north and west of the Ophir Pit, but the limitation of time dictates taking another direction. Suffice it to say that the Comstock has many secrets to yield and it is possible to spend years exploring the various aspects of such a remarkable place. This tour, however, calls for a return to the corner of B and Sutton Streets. A walk to the south along B Street takes the visitor past several substantial houses on the western, uphill side of the street. The conventional rule was that merchants and the "well-to-do" lived on the streets above the commercial corridor of C Street, while the humble miners resided below. This is not entirely true, since the far northern and southern ends of the upper streets housed many laborers and the unemployed frequently squatted in cabins high in the hills during slumps in the economy. Still, the core of B Street preserves several Italianate, Victorian-era houses that would have represented the height of comfort in the 1870s. This area was almost entirely destroyed by the Great Fire of 1875, so most of these buildings date to 1876 or 1877.

3 One notable house, at 58 North B Street, between Union and Sutton, was built by Henry

Piper, the brother of theater impresario John Piper. With its large bay window, the two-story structure was nearly lost to neglect. Hard work, considerable optimism, and the best of preservation practices rescued the historic treasure, which began a new life in the early twenty-first century as a bed-and-breakfast.

4 To the south of the Henry Piper House are brick buildings that recall the importance of the community's fraternal organizations. The Miners' Union Hall, the meeting place of the Knights of Pythias—a fraternal organization that grew out of the Civil War in an effort to heal a wounded nation—and the structure that served the Independent Order of Odd Fellows (IOOF) all stand near the corner of B and Union Streets. The Miners' Union Hall exhibits a metal device that looks like a shield. Originally gilded, the emblem is a beehive, a popular nineteenth-century means to signal collective labor. An earlier hall—destroyed by fire—housed the first public library in Nevada. The Pythian Hall is denoted by the letters "K of P" high on its cornice. Although the exterior has seen better days, the second-floor meeting room is one of the best-preserved interior spaces in the community, with a high ceiling clothed in its original pressed tin. The top of a flagpole standing on the downhill side of B Street, next to the IOOF building, bears the image of three linked chains, an emblem of the order.

4 ■ Masonry buildings

5 Between the Henry Piper House and the Miners" Union Hall is the location of the apartment building where Mark Twain lived with his friend and mentor Dan De Quille. Both were reporters for the *Territorial Enterprise*. A fire destroyed the entire block in the summer of 1863, so the multistory structure was new when Twain and De Quille took up residence there in the autumn. The building disappeared long ago, probably a victim of the 1875 fire like nearly

5 ■ IOOF building

everything else on the block, and modern infill now occupies the site. Twain and De Quille would have walked across B Street to report for duty at the *Territorial Enterprise* building, with newspaper offices on the second floor and other businesses on the lower C Street frontage. Again, the Great Fire of 1875 destroyed this building, like so many others.

Most tourists fail to notice the unimposing B Street facade of the IOOF property, preferring instead to visit Grandma's Fudge. This long-standing institution serves customers from the first floor of the building, facing C Street, operating below where Odd Fellows once met for the betterment of society. The empty lot to the south of the building is the site of a succession of International hotels, structures that either burned or were moved. The 1875 fire consumed an impressive brick edifice, but owners replaced it with a soaring six-story hotel, which opened in 1878. Businesses occupied street-level spaces on both B and C Streets, and the building featured the first public elevator in Nevada. The 1914 fire that destroyed the remarkable hotel burned so hot that it damaged the brick of the Odd Fellows' building, which subsequently needed a layer of concrete for stability. In the 1980s, the owner of the fudge shop realized that the large gray wall was an eyesore that could become a canvas, and so she commissioned a trompe-l'oeil, a highly detailed and accurate painting designed to trick the eye. The depiction of the top and bottom floors of the International Hotel gives visitors a chance to see something of the wonderful institution that once stood there.

6 Piper's Opera House occupies the northwest corner of B and Union Streets. The front of the structure was a business block erected in 1863 by John Piper. His original Old Corner Bar, established in 1860 to the south, burned in the 1863 fire that swept

through the area. Piper decided to build a new home for his saloon and to add space for other businesses and apartments. The brick facade is one of the few remnants from Twain's Virginia City, and Piper's bar became one of the more fashionable places to gather throughout the first two decades of Comstock history. When Piper's Opera House, two blocks downhill on D Street, burned during the fire of 1875, he consolidated his businesses by building a new theater behind his 1863 brick business block, which was charred but still standing. Another fire consumed the theater in 1883, but the persistent theater impresario constructed another new auditorium, opened in 1885. This is the stage that serves patrons to this day. Its interior space is one of the best-preserved examples of its kind in the nation and remains as a testament to the days when Piper's Opera House was a required stop for the most famous performers of the late nineteenth century.

7 While standing on B Street on the south side of Piper's Opera House and looking uphill, it is possible to see the Piper-Beebe House, at 2 South A

Street. Local merchant Arthur F. MacKay (no relation to John Mackay, the silver baron) built the residence after the 1875 fire. John Piper's son Edward purchased the house years later. He resided there with his wife, Lavinia, and their children. After Edward's death in 1907, Lavinia married prizefighter Dan Conner, and they continued to live in the home while operating the theater as best they could in a shrinking economy. When Lucius Beebe and Charles Clegg came to town in the 1940s, they hoped to live in a house with a distinguished pedigree. With typical Comstock disregard for the truth, locals indicated that the MacKay residence belonged to John Piper, a conclusion that they presumably felt was justified because the house had once sheltered Piper's son and grandchildren. The Beebe-Clegg chapter ironically gave the "Piper House" the pedigree that the new owners were hoping to purchase. Beebe and Clegg were noted writers, and with their tenure as the editors of the resuscitated *Territorial Enterprise* of the mid-twentieth century, the house acquired a new layer of historic significance.

7 ■ Storey County Courthouse

Continuing along B Street, crossing Union Street, visitors encounter the large edifice of the Storey County Courthouse. Built in 1876 to replace a predecessor that burned the year before, this was the most expensive county courthouse erected in the first half century of Nevada history. The elaborate Italianate design was the most extravagant of three options proposed by Kenitzer and Raun, a San Francisco architectural firm. One of the building's famous features is an imposing gold-colored statue of Lady Justice. Local folklore has long maintained that she is one of two or three in the nation without a blindfold. A widely publicized survey in the 1980s documented nearly thirty other depictions of the goddess without a blindfold, but the local tradition continues to thrive. Iron trim and Philadelphia brick decorate the front of the courthouse while finely appointed walnut trim and wood-grained paint imitating oak make the interior one of the more impressive spaces in Virginia City. The structure still houses county offices and is open weekdays. This facility is one of two nineteenth-century courthouses still used by county government in Nevada. The other is in Eureka.

8 Directly across the street from the courthouse stands a humble house that would escape the notice of the casual observer. Evidence from the 1880 federal manuscript census indicates, however, that this is one of two surviving Chinese laundries in Virginia City (the other one is on South D Street). During the 1870s, there were dozens of laundries operating in residential neighborhoods. Most were owned by young Chinese men, but some widowed Irish women and others also plied the difficult, backbreaking trade.

9 From the parking lot on the south side of the courthouse, it is possible to see a simple red shed that houses an antique fire hydrant on A Street above.

8 ■ Chinese laundry

9 ■ Apartment building

The community built the structure in the wake of the greatest conflagration in Virginia City's history. With what seems a poetic statement, the small building is across the street from the site of the boardinghouse that caught fire in the early-morning hours of October 26, 1875. This location also provides a good opportunity to look up at the peak of Mount Davidson, reaching 1,600 feet above the town. The deepest Comstock shaft descended 3,200 feet in a straight drop of the elevator. That is twice the height of Mount Davidson, underscoring the scale of the mines that honeycomb the mountainside beneath the community.

On the southeast corner of B and Taylor Streets stands an unremarkable two-story brick building, attached to other masonry structures to the south and east. The Great Fire of 1875 roared down the north side of Taylor, but it did not jump to the south until it was farther downhill. The buildings on the south side of Taylor consequently tend to date to a time before 1875. In the case of the simple brick structure on the corner, the exact date is known: it replaced an apartment building destroyed just before midnight on June 29, 1873. That night, an explosion rocked Virginia City. Jacob Van Bokkelen, the most noted fatality in the disaster, was a local entrepreneur who owned several businesses, including a dynamite importation enterprise. People generally believed the new product to be so safe that storing inventory in a place of residence was not absurd. When Van Bokkelen had too many crates, he was known to sleep on them. For a reason never completely understood, there was a spontaneous detonation, which killed ten people, making it one of the worst industrial accidents in Nevada history. A later inquest focused on Van Bokkelen's pet monkey, which was, perhaps, toying with fuses.

10 Intrepid hikers can tackle the incline of Taylor Street to A Street and the even higher blocks. Most do not walk up to A Street because of the intimidating idea of the ascent. Nevertheless, whether encountered by foot or car, many of the higher streets feature lovely houses of historic importance, offering a reward for the effort. For example, the impressive King Mansion was built around 1870 for a Comstock banker named George Anson King. The imposing house is apparently a survivor of the fire, and several owners followed King. In the 1940s, the mansion served as the Bonanza Inn, a distinguished restaurant patronized by socialites, many of whom were waiting for divorces in Northern Nevada. In 1953, Versal McBride, who founded the Bucket of Blood Saloon in 1931, purchased the mansion and made it his home.

11 Continuing the tour along B Street on the uphill side, a little to the south of the intersection with Taylor, one comes to the building that housed the Virginia and Gold Hill Water Company. The two-story structure was the water master's home and the office for one of the greatest engineering achievements of the West. Beginning in 1873, the water company replaced the rancid local mine water with an importation from the Sierra Nevada. A series of dams, flumes, and tunnels fed an iron pipe that dropped clear, clean mountain water 1,200 feet from the Sierra to the valley floor. Employing the concept of an inverted siphon, the ingenious design relied on pressure to force the precious liquid up into the Virginia Range, where it filled a reservoir above Virginia City. The system—replaced bit by bit over the years—continues to serve the Comstock.

Farther to the south, on the uphill side of B Street, several houses constitute what locals call "Millionaires' Row." Most people who became truly affluent

10 ■ King Mansion

11 ■ Water Company building

WALKING TOUR   **117**

in Virginia City moved elsewhere, and San Francisco had more than its share of mansions for Comstock millionaires. Nothing in Virginia City approached the most opulent examples of wealthy housing that the Nevada mines financed in California. Nevertheless, this part of B Street exhibits some fine homes that served prosperous businessmen. Twentieth-century tourists in search of an expression of the millions in gold and silver would not be denied, and so this group of buildings took on its latter-day name.

12 Notable among the structures of "Millionaires' Row" is the "Castle," home to mine superintendent Robert Graves. This nineteenth-century community leader tried to capture a feeling of grandeur when he built his residence in 1868, although the wooden house, with its Second Empire features, hardly resembles a castle. It is remarkable for its interior lavishness and the degree of its preservation, which includes most of the original furnishings. The house showcases silver doorknobs, etched-glass panels, linen lace curtains from Brussels, Carrara marble fireplaces from Italy, and French mirrors trimmed in gold leaf. In 1887, pharmacist A. M. Cole constructed his mansion to the north of the Castle. This two-story house dates to 1887; Cole lived there until 1914.

To walk down Taylor Street is to follow the edge of the 1875 fire. The buildings on the left, to the north, were within the fire zone, while the ones on the right were undamaged. Recent research demonstrates that many of the masonry structures within the fire zone survived, but there was still a great deal of post-fire construction in Virginia City's core, which experienced most of the damage. Walking north along C Street, one can see many examples of pilasters—the iron columns decorating the fronts of buildings—with

12 ■ The Castle

the date "1876," which commemorated the rebirth of the community as well as the nation's centennial.

13 ■ *Territorial Enterprise* building

13 Just north of Taylor on the eastern, downhill side of C Street is the *Territorial Enterprise* building. It houses an excellently preserved assortment of late-nineteenth-century printing equipment, reflections of the wealth of one of the West's great journalistic institutions. The *Territorial Enterprise* sputtered out of existence with several final issues in the mid-1890s, but its reputation lingered. In the mid-twentieth century, Lucius Beebe and his partner, Charles Clegg, purchased the building and the newspaper, resuscitating the storied publication as a popular weekly. The newcomers also published a book that claimed this was the structure where Samuel Clemens worked and adopted his pen name, Mark Twain. This was not the case. The real history of the surviving *Territorial Enterprise* building is no less significant for want of a direct Twain connection. The institution is so important that its place is permanently etched in the history of American journalism and literature.

To the north, on the uphill side of C Street, the Delta Saloon operates as yet another noteworthy Comstock property. Much of the building collapsed due to an excessive snow load during the early twentieth century. And, of course, the entire block was within the 1875 fire zone. Surviving elements and many period artifacts today comprise the closest thing Virginia City has to a vintage, Nevada-style casino dating to the birth of legal gambling in 1931. Other places have slot machines, but the Delta represents an early attempt to bring Depression-era gambling to the Comstock. The Delta has thrived for so long, it has become historic in its own right.

14 ■ Molinelli's Hotel

15 ■ Red Dog Saloon

14 Farther north on C Street, past the vacant lot that was once the site of the International Hotel, is the Silver Queen, home to a notable saloon. Tourists remember the place for its sixteen-foot painting of a saloon girl—the Silver Queen herself—decorated with 3,261 silver dollars, 28 gold coins, and numerous vintage dimes. She dates from the mid-twentieth century and represents an attempt to distinguish the establishment from its competitors. Even more remarkable, however, is the well-preserved hotel above the saloon. The Molinelli Hotel, built after the 1875 fire, allows visitors to imagine what places like the International Hotel might have looked like. Exquisite halls with natural light descending from skylights provide access to recently restored rooms with high ceilings. Little has changed here since the 1870s.

15 Farther north, also on the uphill side of C Street, is the Red Dog Saloon, an institution of considerable importance during the 1960s. Located at the nineteenth-century site of the Comstock Hotel, the Red Dog featured Bay Area rock bands such as the Charlatans and Big Brother and the Holding Company in 1965. Although the Charlatans never achieved commercial success, the Red Dog's first house band is often credited with giving birth to the San Francisco psychedelic music scene.

Continuing north, on the downhill side, is the Way It Was Museum on the corner of C and Sutton Streets. This institution is a mid-twentieth-century effort to interpret the past to the increasing number of visitors to Virginia City. Little has changed in the museum since it opened in the 1950s. Exhibits include an excellent vintage diagram of underground excavations crafted by an engineer who worked in the mining district. With this remarkable artifact, tourists can better imagine the maze that constituted the Comstock beneath the surface. Hundreds of other objects and photographs add to the quantity of things one can see there.

16 With the immense popularity of the 1960s television show *Bonanza,* many Virginia City property owners rushed to make their businesses look like buildings the fictional Cartwrights would recognize. With its cedar-veneer edifice, the Bonanza Casino on the downhill side of North C Street represents the last survivor of these Cartwright-era modifications. A nineteenth-century building is still visible, peering from behind the disguise, but its "Wild West" twentieth-century facade has its own significance.

17 Returning to the downhill side of C and Union Streets, the visitor should notice the famed Bucket of Blood Saloon. Signage suggests the institution opened in 1876, but this is a reference to the date of the building rather than that of the actual business, which was established in the early 1930s. The structure itself is a fire survivor that witnessed several periods of construction, but it was remodeled after 1875 and became home to two narrow saloons. The owner of the Bucket of Blood removed the wall separating the bars, creating a spacious interior and a business that is frequently voted the best rural saloon in Nevada.

16 ∎ Bonanza Casino

Behind and below the Bucket of Blood, beneath a parking lot facing D Street, is the site of the Boston Saloon, an African American establishment that operated at this location between 1866 and 1875. In comparing this establishment with several other excavated saloons, archaeologists determined that this dignified business had some of the best cuts of meat, the finest crystal, and the cleanest gas lighting. William A. G. Brown, the Massachusetts native and freeborn owner of the saloon, eventually purchased several lots throughout town.

17 ∎ Bucket of Blood Saloon

Beginning in the twentieth century, the central part of D Street was promoted as the town's red-light district. In fact, its story was much more complex. In the 1860s and 1870s, city ordinances restricted prostitutes to the few downtown blocks of D Street, but there were many other institutions here that had nothing to do with sexual commerce. Besides the Boston Saloon, the Frederick House on the northwest corner of D and Union Streets catered to the wealthiest of patrons. It is still possible to see the brick wall of the lowest level of the Frederick House, now mostly demolished, but once standing on the north side of Union. The building dominated the block between C and D Streets.

Across D Street on the downhill side and to the south about a hundred feet from the Boston Saloon is the site of Maguire's Opera House, one of the finest theaters in the West, opened in 1863. Thomas Maguire established a Virginia City tradition of importing the world's best acts. In 1867, he sold his business to John Piper, who perpetuated the high theatrical standards, earning a significant place for the institution in the history of the American stage. The Great Fire of 1875 destroyed the theater. After the fire, Piper rebuilt his auditorium uphill at the corner of B and Union, and the reputation of the Opera House persisted.

During the 1860s, near the northeast corner of D and Union, a row of humble buildings served as "cribs" for independent, self-employed prostitutes. These women were distinct from their sisters who worked in one of several Virginia City brothels, upscale places that demanded a cut of the profits in return for a degree of safety. One of the freelancers was Julia Bulette, who was murdered during the early-morning hours of January 20, 1867. A year later, authorities arrested a French immigrant named Jean Millain, accusing him of the murder. Thanks to a well-publicized trial that resulted in a guilty verdict and Virginia City's first public hanging, Millain gave Bulette a boost in local lore. Decades later, she would be remembered as the wealthiest and the kindest of prostitutes, a biography that gave her a far grander life than what she enjoyed in reality.

Farther down Union, centering on H Street, Chinese immigrants built a place they called home. At its height, Chinatown housed more than a thousand residents, and its stores, doctors, restaurants, and opium dens attracted non-Asians who were intrepid enough to venture along the streets and alleyways to experience the exotic. The neighborhood burned in 1875, and although the Chinese rebuilt their community, later fires destroyed all remaining structures. Bottle diggers—trespassing on private property—subsequently damaged much of what survived, depriving later generations of the opportunity to learn about this unfairly maligned group.

At the bottom of Union Street, but quite visible from the upper reaches of town, stands the imposing brick structure that housed St. Mary Louise Hospital. In 1876, the Daughters of Charity of Saint Vincent de Paul opened their four-story hospital at the base of Six Mile Canyon. Mary Louise Mackay, wife of silver king John Mackay, donated the land for the facility, which had the capacity to serve seventy patients. In addition to their hospital, the Daughters ran a Virginia City orphanage and school, both long gone. The order left the Comstock in 1897, having served the community since 1864. St. Mary's Art and Retreat Center now occupies the restored building and grounds.

18 The corner of Taylor and D Streets represents the southern edge of the red-light district. The Methodist church on the southeast corner catered to the substantial Cornish population. Today, Virginia

City Middle School—including its New Deal–era core—occupies the site. To the south several hoisting works, lifting cages full of men and ore up and down shafts, made this a noisy center of industry. Downhill on Taylor are two of the community's surviving nineteenth-century churches, including St. Mary in the Mountains. The large size of the Catholic institution reflects the fact that nearly a third of the community was Irish or Irish American by the 1880 census. To this day, many descendants continue to attend this place of worship, which has one of the more elegant and well-preserved interiors of nineteenth-century Nevada churches.

The neighboring church, St. Paul's, served the Episcopal congregation, which was smaller. Still, the little wooden Gothic Revival building also has a charming interior that captures an image of life in the 1870s. Earlier churches dedicated to Saint Mary and Saint Paul were victims of the 1875 fire. Both congregations were able to reuse the lower levels of masonry that survived the devastation, and their institutions reopened in grand style before the close of the 1870s.

Downhill from Washington Street is an area that Irish immigrants once dominated. Living in houses along streets radiating north and south from Washington, these residents were able to maintain a sense of community, anchored by the Catholic church and by the Daughters of Charity, who operated their orphanage and school between H and I Streets, south of Washington.

19 Underneath E Street in front of the Catholic church, dozens of trains rumbled through a tunnel each day, bringing passengers and goods to the center of town. To the north sprawled a rail yard that accommodated the traffic. Remnants include the large expanse of level ground—an anomaly in this hillside town—as well as the old freight barn, one of the last of the surviving treasures associated with the Virginia and Truckee Railroad.

20 The Comstock History Center, the large yellow building on the corner of Union and E Streets, opened in 2005, but it features nineteenth-century architectural elements from the railroad, including the design of a car shed that stood about fifty feet to the north. Inside, the Dayton (#18), a rare Virginia and Truckee Railroad locomotive, rests on rails located where earlier counterparts once served this important lifeline to the outside world. The engine is one of two survivors of the Central Pacific shops in Sacramento, and it starred in several Hollywood films. The massive doors that allow the engine to roll in and out are exact replicas of those once belonging to the Carson City V&T shops before the demolition of that structure in 1991.

21 To resume a tour of C Street, the main commercial corridor, walk up Taylor from the two churches. Taylor and C Streets accommodated the most important financial institutions of the mining

19 ■ V&T Freight Barn

20 ■ Comstock History Center

district. The Bank of California building stood on the southwest, uphill corner of the intersection, housing the economic hub of the Comstock for almost a decade beginning in 1864. Under the direction of bank president William Ralston and his assistant William Sharon, the Bank of California commanded a monopoly of the district's mines and mills. With that source of funds, the bank supported extravagant projects in California's Bay Area. When others began to erode the control of the bank, the fabric of its existence cracked, and eventually its monopoly collapsed. Today the building serves as a saloon. Its first floor features an excellent mine tour that extends into the mountainside at the site of the Best and Belcher Mine, the location of the Big Bonanza. While this is a re-creation of a mine, it is a well done one. A sign for the Sharon House recalls the restaurant that once occupied the second floor and was a local favorite.

21 ■ Bank of California building

22 Across the street, on the southeast corner of Taylor and C Streets, the Nevada Bank occupied part of the Pinschower Building, which dates to 1862, the year after Nevada became a territory. Jacob Pinschower built his large masonry structure to house a variety of businesses. The wide doorway at the center of the building accommodated carriages, and below there are stalls for the horses of wealthy patrons who would call for a vehicle to be delivered for trips about town or elsewhere. A decade later, the northern end of the building would become the Virginia City office for Nevada Bank of San Francisco. Founded by the Bonanza Firm and led by silver barons John Mackay and James Fair, the Nevada Bank proved too formidable for the Ralston-Sharon monopoly. After the discovery of the Big Bonanza in 1873, Mackay and his associates were able to wrest control from the Bank of

22 ■ Pinschower Building

California, pointing Virginia City and the mining district in a new direction.

23 The west side of C Street, heading south, includes some of Virginia City's earliest structures. The Washoe Club—originally the Douglass Building—was constructed in 1862 at the same time as the Pinschower Building. The elegant saloon on the main floor was named the Crystal Bar for its fine chandeliers. After the 1875 fire, the Washoe Club, also known as the Millionaires' Club, moved into the second story of the Douglass Building, above the saloon. This membership-only society provided a retreat for the wealthiest Comstock mine owners and investors. The club offered a variety of services—a restaurant, saloon, reading room, and hotel—all far removed from the average man on the street.

23 ■ Douglass Building

24 In the twentieth century, the Crystal Bar, together with its ceiling fixtures, moved to the northwest corner of C and Taylor, where it now serves as the Virginia City Visitor Center. At that point, the name of the defunct Washoe Club became associated with the business on the main floor of the Douglass Building, where it is used to this day. Numerous television shows have celebrated the institution, not for its remarkable degree of preservation but rather for the ghosts that are reputed to haunt the place. A wooden spiral staircase to the rear—noteworthy because of the height it achieves without support—has been the focus of many reported apparitions.

24 ■ Crystal Bar

25 On the east side of the street, an old brick building is now the home of the Comstock Firemen's Museum. This structure boasts a construction date of 1862. It originally housed a grocery store and then became a saloon for a while. In 1934, the community put it to use as a fire station, removing one of

25 ■ Comstock Firemen's Museum

26 ■ Business building

27 ■ Presbyterian Church

the center brick pillars so trucks could come and go. Abandoned in 1962, the building began a new life in 1979 as a museum devoted to the story of those who risked their lives fighting fires on the Comstock.

26 Farther south, on the west side of the street, stand single-story brick buildings that may be some of the oldest in town, dating to the very founding of Virginia City between 1859 and 1861. They exhibit a crude but substantial approach to architecture, with a tall brick first story capped with a decorative but simple masonry corbels supporting wooden gables. Of note are original metal awnings that have been cut in an undulating pattern to imitate canvas. Several of the structures, which originally housed shops of various sorts, still have bay windows used to display goods more effectively to passersby.

27 The 1867 wooden First Presbyterian Church is the oldest surviving religious structure in town. Standing farther to the south on the uphill side of South C Street, the church was outside the fire zone and thus survived the 1875 devastation. The edifice erected for Presbyterians is small and inexpensive because it served the Scottish community in a day when many religions were linked entirely to ethnicity. The Scottish Americans were too few in Virginia City to support a grand structure, so their church, still standing after all the intervening years, was a modest presence located at the south end of C Street where real estate was less expensive. The interior has gone through many changes since 1867, but a devoted congregation strives to restore its historic appearance.

To the south of the Presbyterian church was a district known as the Barbary Coast, a rough part of town where danger, drugs, and murder lurked. Echoing San Francisco's area with the same name, the term came from North Africa, where early-nineteenth-century

America fought the War of the Barbary Pirates as the young republic attempted to protect its shipping in the Mediterranean. Towns with areas named after the Barbary Coast were recognizing the shared sense of danger. Little remains of Virginia City's Barbary Coast, which clung especially to the uphill, western side of the street. The buildings were so poorly constructed that most fell down. Today, only a few masonry remnants can be seen in the hillside, surviving tenaciously as standing ruins. For the most part, this neighborhood is dominated by pastel-colored cottages moved to Virginia City from American Flat in the 1920s.

28 On the east side of C Street, along the Barbary Coast, it is possible to see large structures that face D Street below. These include a building that is prominently labeled as the "Mackay Mansion," named for silver baron John Mackay. The structure served the Gould and Curry's mine superintendent as his house and office, a place where he could supervise the nearby hoisting works. The two-story brick edifice dates to 1861 and claims to feature the first flush toilet in Nevada Territory. George Hearst was a principal

28 ■ Mackay Mansion

owner of the mine during the construction of this building. By rights, it could be called the Hearst Mansion, although its designation would more properly refer to the Gould and Curry. John Mackay eventually had a controlling interest in the mine, but he probably lived in the mansion for only a few months after the 1875 fire burned his house on B Street. He subsequently moved into an apartment in the International Hotel after it reopened in 1877.

29 Farther south on the west side of D Street is the Savage Mansion, with its Second Empire mansard roof peering high enough that it is clearly visible from C Street. The Savage Mansion also dates to the early 1860s, and it too served as a mine superintendent's home and office. President Grant and his family stayed there when their world tour brought them to the Comstock in 1879. The D Street "mansions," as they are now called, were associated with some of the more prosperous Comstock claims, and each had hoisting works nearby. Most mines began with shafts several blocks uphill, but in the early 1860s, when it became clear that the ore body slanted downhill, the companies began sinking lower shafts along D Street to intercept the lode.

29 ■ Savage Mansion

30 One of the more remarkable stories associated with this transition is linked to the Chollar Mansion, located behind the imposing Fourth Ward School. The Chollar Mine originally had a hoisting work and shaft situated high on the mountain. Today, its former location would hover in midair near the top of the scar left by the Loring Pit, the historic surface excavation on C Street to the west of the Fourth Ward School. In 1871, the company decided to move the two-story brick superintendent's home and office downhill four blocks to its present location. The elegant Chollar Mansion is a testament not only to the wealth of the

30 ■ Chollar Mansion

Comstock, but also to the skill of its workers and engineers who managed a move what would have been a challenge in any century.

Also high on the hill, where Howard Street once extended south from Taylor, was a neighborhood known as Cornish Row. The immigrants from Cornwall, in the far southwest of Britain, were some of the most experienced miners in the world, having developed tin and then copper mines for thousands of years. Although they numbered only about one thousand on the Comstock—fewer than the Irish, for example—they commanded respect and easily claimed the best jobs. While the Irish dominated several Virginia City neighborhoods, many of the Cornish preferred Gold Hill and the Divide, the area between the two communities. Cornish Row, on the southwestern edge of Virginia City, was part of the transition into the Cornish zone. Unfortunately, the last of the houses succumbed during a mid-twentieth-century fire on the hillside.

31 ■ Fourth Ward School

31 One of the most dramatic survivors on the southern edge of Virginia City is the Fourth Ward School, a grand four-story Second Empire wooden building that is the last example of its kind still standing in the nation. Built in 1876 as a tribute to America's centennial, the structure, in the town's Fourth Ward voting district, featured innovations including state-of-the-art ventilation and heating systems, individual desks for each student, and indoor plumbing with flush toilets. The school offered Nevada's first high school diplomas. As the Comstock fell on hard times during the Great Depression of the 1930s, so did the Fourth Ward School. Outdated and with dwindling enrollment, the building closed in 1936. Fifty years later, the structure reopened as an award-winning museum with numerous exhibits devoted to Comstock history. Today, after several

32 ■ Combination Shaft

decades of meticulous preservation efforts and the addition of an extensive archive and research center, visitors can journey back to the school days of the nineteenth century when the institution boasted many educational "firsts." A tour of the Comstock is incomplete without a visit to the interior of this grand structure.

32 Looking from the east windows of the Historic Fourth Ward School Museum, visitors can view the ruins of the Combination Shaft with its large mine dump dominating the hill on the south side of the ravine. This site preserves one of the last attempts of the 1880s to locate a viable ore body that would sustain the community. Beyond the Combination Shaft, the site of one of Virginia City's original cemeteries occupies the side of the hill. Despite twentieth-century efforts to label the area as a "Boot Hill," many of the town's early residents—including the friends of Julia Bulette—made "the long, last walk" to lay to rest loved ones in the Flowery Cemetery, which was a perfectly respectable burial ground. In the late 1860s, Virginia City's town fathers designated a new, closer graveyard at the north end of E Street. Like many of their Victorian counterparts throughout the nation, the Silver Terrace Cemeteries allowed mourners to stroll through lush gardens. The graves located there reflect the town's mining roots, ethnic diversity, and deep ties to religious and fraternal organizations. Today the gardens are gone, but the Comstock Cemetery Foundation's continuing restoration efforts preserve the final resting place of those who contributed to Comstock greatness.

Farther down Six Mile Canyon rises Sugar Loaf, a solitary hill that has long served as a local natural landmark. In fact, Sugar Loaf is a volcanic plug, the interior of a millennia-old solidified core of a volcano, its magma long since cooled. This outcropping recalls the geological turmoil that created the Comstock and left its remarkable gold and silver deposits.

Additional Features

Of course, Virginia City is not the only Comstock community. To the south, on State Route 342, is Gold Hill, which features the Gold Hill Hotel that dates to the early 1860s. Above the hotel are two hoisting works associated with the Yellow Jacket Mine, scene of the infamous 1869 disaster that unfolded as the worst industrial accident in Nevada history. The hoist directly behind the Gold Hill Hotel is likely the oldest one still standing on the Comstock, perhaps dating to the mid-1860s.

Besides these, there are many other historic structures in this community, which once served as home to 8,000 people. South of Gold Hill, the natural rock buttress called Devil's Gate separates Storey and Lyon Counties. On the north side of Devil's Gate is a twenty-first-century open pit. As mining evolved over

Yellow Jacket Mine

Silver City

the decades, the evidence of its activities has changed. While the pit is larger than its nineteenth-century counterparts, there is continuity: the industry has repeatedly altered the landscape.

Devil's Gate represents the northern limit of Silver City, founded in 1859. This town never knew the affluence of Virginia City, and so its structures tend toward the modest. Outside the typical trail of the tourist, Silver City's economy is distinct from those of its northern Comstock siblings. Nevertheless, Silver City retains its own character and has many evocative historic buildings. Perhaps most notably, its cemetery includes the grave of Hosea Grosh, one of the first prospectors to realize that silver dominated the area. Some of the best mining resources in the district—everything from mills to hoisting works from many different periods of Comstock mining—survive from Gold Hill to Silver City.

To the southeast of Silver City, the original wagon road extended to Dayton, but today that route is barely passable. The paved road, which is the only safe way to reach US 50, extends to the southwest of Silver City. From the intersection with US 50, travelers may reach Dayton by heading east for about three miles. Dayton, one of the oldest settlements in Nevada, dates to the early 1850s. The main street and its Odeon Hall, a large masonry structure, are among the notable treasures of the Comstock Historic District.

Old Town Dayton has been overshadowed by growth on the east side of the Carson River, but the historic core of the community features several impressive nineteenth-century buildings. Farther along Highway 50 to the north and east, the traveler passes the site of the Sutro Tunnel, nestled on the hillside above the river plain. Since the Sutro Tunnel site is on private property, tourists are not allowed except during rare special events, but when opportunities occur, this place is worth the visit.

Dayton

In many ways, the Comstock does not end with these closely connected communities. The Virginia and Truckee Railroad linked Virginia City with Carson City and its United States Mint, which is now home to the Nevada State Museum. Comstock miners constructed one of the nation's best exhibits on underground mining in the basement of the museum, and anyone interested in Comstock history must include a visit to this marvel. But the legendary mining district's past is also entwined with that of Lake Tahoe and much of the Sierra, which continue to deal with the effects of Comstock-era lumbering.

To the north in Washoe Valley are a number of locations that are key to the Comstock story. None is more celebrated than Bowers Mansion, which is now a Washoe County Regional Park. Bowers Mansion dates to 1863 and was home to Sandy and Eilley Bowers, who became millionaires thanks to a Gold Hill claim.

Bowers Mansion

Statue of John Mackay

When their mine failed and Sandy died, Eilley was left to struggle financially. This well-preserved icon survives as the largest house built during Nevada's territorial period, and it owes its existence to the earliest period of Comstock wealth.

Similarly, Reno's aptly named Virginia Street extends from the north to the south and eventually to Geiger Grade, the road that leads to the Comstock. The fact that this main thoroughfare still retains the name of the capital of mining recalls a time when Virginia City was the most important community in Nevada. The old quad of the University of Nevada's Reno campus on North Virginia Street is crowned by the Mackay School of Mines building. Funding for the institution came from Clarence Mackay, the son of the Irish miner who struck it rich with the Big Bonanza in 1873. In front of the building is a 1908 bronze statue of John Mackay, crafted by Gutzon Borglum, the artist who went on to carve Mount Rushmore. Mackay stands in his simple miner's clothes, leaning on his pick and peering to the southeast toward Virginia City. The connections throughout the region run deep.

A final word needs to be said about archaeology. The Virginia City National Historic Landmark has been devastated by decades of bottle digging. People searching for keepsakes or treasures have destroyed much of the potential for reading the past with careful, scientific excavation. Nevertheless, a great deal remains, and professional excavations teach the public much about life in the past. Archaeologists from the University of Nevada, Reno have uncovered hundreds of thousands of artifacts from the Comstock. They have also welcomed tens of thousands of visitors to excavations, announced findings to an eager public, and sponsored exhibits and books that allow everyone to enjoy the benefits of the resource. It is important

All photographs in the Walking Tour by Ronald M. James

to be respectful of the archaeological treasures that remain in this national landmark. Those who dig for artifacts without permission in the district are stealing from private property owners or public agencies, and trespassers can be prosecuted. Visitors are asked to respect the Virginia City National Historic Landmark. It is a treasure of international stature, and it deserves to be preserved.

Selected Bibliography

Basso, Dave. *The Washoe Club: The Story of a Great Social Institution.* Sparks, Nev.: Falcon Hill, 1988.

BeDunnah, Gary P. "A History of the Chinese in Nevada: 1855–1904." Master's thesis, University of Nevada, Reno, 1966.

Belasco David. *Gala Days of Piper's Opera House and the California Theater.* Reprint, Sparks, Nev.: Falcon Hill Press, 1991.

Berlin, Ellin. *Silver Platter.* London: Hammond, 1958.

Butler, Anne M. "Mission in the Mountains: The Daughters of Charity in Virginia City." In *Comstock Women: The Making of a Mining Community,* edited by Ronald M. James and C. Elizabeth Raymond, 142–64. Reno: University of Nevada Press, 1998. Hereafter cited as James and Raymond, *Comstock Women.*

Carter, Gregg Lee. "Social Demography of the Chinese in Nevada, 1870–1880." *Nevada Historical Society Quarterly* 18 (Summer 1975): 73–90.

Chan, Loren D. "The Chinese in Nevada: An Historical Survey, 1856–1970." *Nevada Historical Society Quarterly* 25 (Winter 1982): 266–314.

Chung, Sue Fawn. "Their Changing World: Chinese Women on the Comstock, 1860–1910." In James and Raymond, *Comstock Women,* 203–28.

Clark, Walter Van Tilburg, ed. *The Journals of Alfred Doten, 1849–1903.* Reno: University of Nevada Press, 1973.

Clemens, Samuel [Mark Twain, pseud.]. *Roughing It.* Edited by Harriet Elinor Smith and Edgar Marquess Branch. Berkeley: University of California Press, 1993. Originally published 1872.

De Quille, Dan. See Wright, William.

Dixon, Kelly J. *Boomtown Saloons: Archaeology and History in Virginia City.* Reno: University of Nevada Press, 2005.

Drury, Wells. *An Editor on the Comstock Lode.* Palo Alto, Calif.: Pacific Books, 1948.

Emmons, David. *The Butte Irish: Class and Ethnicity in an American Mining Town, 1875–1925.* Urbana: University of Illinois Press, 1989.

Gavazzi, Italo. "American Flat: Stepchild of the Comstock Lode—Part I." *Nevada Historical Society Quarterly* 41, no. 2 (Summer 1998): 92–101.

Goldman, Marion S. *Gold Diggers and Silver Miners: Prostitution and Social Life on the Comstock Lode.* Reno: University of Nevada Press, 1981.

Hardesty, Donald L. "Gender and Archaeology on the Comstock." In James and Raymond, *Comstock Women,* 283–302.

——. *Mining Archaeology in the American West: A View from the Silver State.* Lincoln: University of Nebraska Press, 2010.

Hattori, Eugene M. "'And Some of Them Swear like Pirates': Acculturation of American Indian Women in Nineteenth-Century Virginia City." In James and Raymond, *Comstock Women,* 229–45.

——. *Northern Paiutes on the Comstock: Archaeology and Ethno-history of an American Indian Population in Virginia City, Nevada.* Carson City: Nevada State Museum, 1975.

Highton, Jake. *Nevada Newspaper Days: A History of Journalism in the Silver State.* Stockton, Calif.: Heritage West Books, 1990.

James, Ronald M. "Defining the Group: Nineteenth-Century Cornish on the Mining Frontier." In *Cornish Studies 2,* edited by Philip Payton, 32–47. Exeter, UK: University of Exeter Press, 1994.

——. "Erin's Daughters on the Comstock: Building Community." In James and Raymond, *Comstock Women,* 246–62.

——. "Home Away from Home: Cornish Immigrants in Nineteenth-Century Nevada," In *Cornish Studies 15,* edited by Philip Payton, 141–63. Exeter, UK: University of Exeter Press, 2008.

——. "Mark Twain's Virginia City: The 1864 Bird's Eye View of Grafton Brown." *Nevada Historical Society Quarterly* 51, no. 2 (Summer 2008): 140–47.

——. "On the Edge of the Big Bonanza: Declining Fortunes and the Comstock Lode." *Mining History Journal* 3 (1996): 101–8.

——. *The Roar and the Silence: A History of Virginia City and the Comstock Lode.* Reno: University of Nevada Press, 1998.

——. "Timothy Francis McCarthy: Life of an Irish Immigrant Worker on the Comstock." *Nevada Historical Society Quarterly* 39, no. 4 (Winter 1996): 300–8.

James, Ronald M., with Richard D. Adkins and Rachel J. Hartigan. "Competition and Coexistence in the Wash House: A View of the Comstock from the Bottom of the Laundry Pile." *Western Historical Quarterly* 25, no. 2 (Summer 1994): 165–84.

James, Ronald M., and Michael J. Brodhead. "The 1861 Bird's Eye View of Grafton Brown." *Nevada Historical Society Quarterly* 49, no. 1 (Spring 2006): 43–54.

James, Ronald M., and Kenneth H. Fliess. "Women of the Mining West: Virginia City Revisited." In James and Raymond, *Comstock Women*, 17–39.

James, Ronald M., and C. Elizabeth Raymond, eds. *Comstock Women: The Making of a Mining Community.* Reno: University of Nevada Press, 1998.

James, Susan A. "Julia Bulette's Probate Records." In *Uncovering Nevada's Past: A Primary Source History of the Silver State,* edited by John B. Reid and Ronald M. James, 55–59. Reno: University of Nevada Press, 2004.

———. "Queen of Tarts." *Nevada Magazine,* September–October 1984, 51–53.

———. "Shakespeare and Bear Fights." *Nevada Magazine,* May–June 2001, 20–23.

———. *Virginia City's Fourth Ward School: From Pride to Glory.* Virginia City: Fourth Ward School Museum, 2003.

Kendall, Robert E. "American Flat: Stepchild of the Comstock Lode—Part II." *Nevada Historical Society Quarterly* 41, no. 2 (Summer 1998): 102–14.

Lewis, Oscar. *Silver Kings: The Lives and Times of Mackay, Fair, Flood, and O'Brien, Lords of the Nevada Comstock Lode.* Reno: University of Nevada Press, 1986.

Lingenfelter, Richard E., and Karen Rix Gash. *The Newspapers of Nevada: A History and Bibliography, 1854–1979.* Reno: University of Nevada Press, 1984.

Lord, Eliot. *Comstock Mining and Miners.* San Diego: Howell-North, 1959. Originally published 1883.

Loverin, Janet I., and Robert A. Nylen. "Creating a Fashionable Society: Comstock Needlework from 1860 to 1880." In James and Raymond, *Comstock Women, 115–41.*

Mack, Effe Mona [Zeke Daniels, pseud.]. Illustrated by Ben Christy. *The Life and Death of Julia C. Bulette, "Queen of the Red Lights": Virginia City, Nevada.* Virginia City: Lamp Post, 1958.

Makley, Michael, *The Infamous King of the Comstock: William Sharon and the Gilded Age in the West.* Reno: University of Nevada Press, 2006.

———. *John Mackay: Silver King in the Gilded Age.* Reno: University of Nevada Press, 2009.

Mathews, Mary McNair. *Ten Years in Nevada or Life in the Pacific Coast.* Lincoln: University of Nebraska Press, 1985. Originally published 1880.

Memmott, Margo. "The Archaeology Beneath Piper's Opera House: A Study of a Nineteenth-Century American Performance Hall." Master's thesis, University of Nevada, Reno, 2004.

Pickering, Lee Lukes. *The Story of St. Mary's Art Center—Now—and St. Mary Louise Hospital—Then.* Carson City: N.p., 1986.

Reid, John B., and Ronald M. James, eds. *Uncovering Nevada's Past: A Primary Source History of the Silver State*. Reno: University of Nevada Press, 2004.

Shepperson, Wilbur S. *Restless Strangers: Nevada's Immigrants and Their Interpreters*. Reno: University of Nevada Press, 1970.

Shinn, Charles Howard. *The Story of the Mine: As Illustrated by the Great Comstock Lode of Nevada*. New York: D. Appleton, 1910.

Smith, Grant, with new material by Joseph V. Tingley. *The History of the Comstock Lode, 1850–1997*. Reno: Nevada Bureau of Mines and Geology in association with the University of Nevada Press, 1998.

Twain, Mark. See Clemens, Samuel.

Waldorf, John Taylor, with Dolores Waldorf Bryant, eds. *A Kid on the Comstock: Reminiscences of a Virginia City Childhood*. Reno: University of Nevada Press, 1991.

Watson, Margaret G. *Silver Theatre: Amusements of Nevada's Mining Frontier, 1850–1864*. Glendale, Calif.: Arthur C. Clark, 1964.

West, Elliott. *The Saloon on the Rocky Mountain Mining Frontier*. Lincoln: University of Nebraska Press, 1979.

Wright, William [Dan De Quille, pseud.]. *The Big Bonanza*. New York: Alfred A. Knopf, 1947. Originally published 1876.

Zanjani, Sally. *Devils Will Reign: How Nevada Began*. Reno: University of Nevada Press, 2006.

Index